Undergraduate
Writing
in Psychology

Undergraduate
Writing
in Psychology

LEARNING TO TELL THE SCIENTIFIC STORY

REVISED EDITION

R. Eric Landrum

American Psychological Association • Washington, DC

Published by
American Psychological Association
750 First Street, NE
Washington, DC 20002
www.apa.org

Fourth Printing, October 2017

To order
APA Order Department
P.O. Box 92984
Washington, DC 20090-2984
Tel: (800) 374-2721; Direct: (202) 336-5510
Fax: (202) 336-5502; TDD/TTY: (202) 336-6123
Online: www.apa.org/pubs/books/
E-mail: order@apa.org

In the U.K., Europe, Africa, and the Middle East, copies may be ordered from
American Psychological Association
3 Henrietta Street
Covent Garden, London
WC2E 8LU England

Typeset in Meridien by Circle Graphics, Columbia, MD

Printer: Edwards Brothers Malloy, Lillington, NC
Cover Designer: Naylor Design, Washington, DC

The opinions and statements published are the responsibility of the author, and such opinions and statements do not necessarily represent the policies of the American Psychological Association.

Library of Congress Cataloging-in-Publication Data

Landrum, R. Eric.
  Undergraduate writing in psychology : learning to tell the scientific story /
R. Eric Landrum. — Rev. ed.
     p. cm.
  Includes bibliographical references and index.
  ISBN 978-1-4338-1216-3 — ISBN 1-4338-1216-9 1.
Psychology—Authorship—Study and teaching. I. Title.
  BF76.7.L36 2012
  808.06'615—dc23
                              2012013682

British Library Cataloguing-in-Publication Data
A CIP record is available from the British Library.

Printed in the United States of America
Revised Edition

*Dedicated to all psychology students
learning to write scientifically
and
to Allison and Scott*

Contents

4

How to Write Your Psychology Paper With Style:
General Tips   53

5

Bringing the Audience Up to Speed With Literature Reviews   89

6

Telling an Original Story Through a Research Paper   105

7

The Rest of the Story: Title, Abstract, References, and Tables   133

8

Reshaping Your Story for Different Audiences: Other Types of Writing in Psychology 163

Preface

As you read this book, one of the key ideas that you will encounter is the notion that it is important for the writer to write for his or her audience. If you are an undergraduate psychology student reading this book, congratulations—YOU are my audience! Simply put, I wrote this book for you. Why in the world would I go and do a thing like that?

I have to admit that I did not wake up one day and say to myself, "Hey, I think I'll write a book about scientific writing today." Actually, the origins of this book lay in my teaching, especially my undergraduate research methods course. As a student, you take these individual courses that accumulate credits, and as long as you take enough courses to satisfy your institution's requirements, you receive your bachelor's degree. From my perspective, however, these individual courses are much more important than that. For example, the research methods course is my way to demonstrate to students how psychologists think, formulate questions, construct answers, and communicate with one another. Your courses should help model the thinking patterns and cognitions of those in the discipline you are studying. This book, although about writing scientifically, is also about modeling the process of how psychologists think and express their thinking in writing.

You have probably already read (or will soon) your share of journal articles in psychology. As you know, they can be difficult to read and comprehend, but I am telling you that it does not have to be this way. Fundamentally, a journal article is about telling a story, and this storytelling notion is the central, underlying theme of this book. You might not understand every nuance of a journal article or book chapter, but if it is well written, you should be able to extract the gist of the

---

This book has been revised and updated to comply with the sixth edition of the *Publication Manual of the American Psychological Association* (APA, 2010).

story. My goal in this book is to teach you this scientific storytelling process. It is also important to remember that good stories are not boring, and they stick with us!

Before telling your story, however, you have to do your research, and this book gives specific examples of how to do that, too. You will find that no matter what area of psychology you are interested in, being able to write is key. Writing scientifically may seem like a tedious task—and let's face it, some aspects of scientific writing, such as formatting your references in American Psychological Association (APA) format, are tedious—but the tasks are more important than you might imagine. The ability to write scientifically is essential if you want to learn to think like a psychologist!

Undoubtedly you have many sources of information about writing available to you, such as your instructors, chapters of selected books, the *Publication Manual,* the writing center on your campus, and so forth. This book is a supplement to all of those sources. It takes some practice to learn to write scientifically, and this book should be most helpful to you as you take those initial steps, particularly because I have modeled the writing process for you, with multiple examples from real students. The more sources of information you have, and the more resources you can call on, the easier and more comfortable you should be as you develop and hone your scientific writing skills.

In the same vein, multiple individuals have been particularly helpful in providing information and resources to help make this book happen. I am grateful to Carol Pack and Naiara Arozamena, former students of mine who agreed to have actual drafts and final versions of their research methods papers reproduced in this book. Because of their generosity, you get to see actual work in first draft, edited, and revised form.

I am especially appreciative of Linda Malnasi McCarter, acquisitions editor at APA Books, who saw value in this project from the very beginning and demonstrated confidence that this book could be a success. If not for Linda's initiative to develop resources to assist undergraduate psychology students, this resource would not exist. I thank Linda for her vote of confidence in me, and I also support Linda's philosophy of providing invaluable resources for undergraduate psychology students. Another key person whom I wish to thank is Susan Herman, development editor at APA Books. Susan provided insightful advice on improving every aspect of the book you are now reading. She reviewed every page of the initial and subsequent manuscripts with a precise eye and an encouraging style. I truly appreciate the efforts of Dan Brachtesende at APA Books. Not only did he champion the toughest permissions to secure, but I appreciate his line-by-line attention to this final manuscript. Be assured that I am fully responsible for the final product you hold here, but Susan's and Dan's attention to detail is an essential factor in any success this book may achieve. Without these efforts, this book would not exist in this form.

Undergraduate
Writing
in Psychology

Introduction

f you are an undergraduate psychology student reading this introduction, this book is for YOU. In the course of your undergraduate career, you will be asked to write papers for a number of different psychology classes. Sometimes you will be asked to write a term paper or lab report; other times you may be asked to write a research paper, either summarizing the available research on a topic, such as a literature review, or about your own original research. This book is designed to help you write scientifically. One of the features I like most about this book—and that I hope you will like, too— is that it includes actual examples of the different steps involved in scientific writing. For example, when I discuss the notecard method and relevant software programs for extracting information from sources, you will see actual notecards. When reviewing how to write the introduction section of a research paper, you will see an actual student's rough draft, an edited version (like it would be corrected by an instructor), and a final draft. In reviewing American Psychological Association (APA) format, you'll be able to quiz yourself about it and see multiple examples of different types of citations you might need to use in your own scientific writing. This book is all about the process of scientific writing and providing you with information and examples about how to do it well.

Although I wrote this book in a linear fashion, you don't have to read it that way. In chapter 1, I start off by establishing the underlying theme of the entire book, that is, that the best communicators in science must be able to tell a good story. As human beings, we enjoy good stories, and we are likely to remember good stories. Chapter 1 provides an overview of the book and briefly reviews the types of assignments for which this book can be most helpful, namely literature reviews and research papers. The importance of identifying your audience and writing for your audience is presented in chapter 1 and also stressed throughout the book.

Before you can jump in and do any type of scientific writing, careful planning needs to occur, and this is the central topic of chapter 2. The development of a clear topic and research question (or thesis statement) is essential to laying the foundation on which your scientific writing will be built. I review library search strategies and available resources and emphasize the importance of meeting the requirements of the assignment, making sure you don't waste time or effort in writing a great paper that doesn't satisfy the demands of the assignment. In chapter 3, I continue with the next steps of the research process, primarily focusing on identifying key resources and discussing methods for extracting information from those sources. I include a detailed description of how you can track information from multiple sources that will facilitate the actual writing process and the synthesis of information from your multiple sources.

In chapter 4, I present some general tips that will apply to most situations in which you are asked to write scientifically in psychology. Key components of this chapter include detailed instructions on creating your first draft, editing, revising, and proofreading. In my discussion of plagiarism, I provide actual examples of text and point out the differences between plagiarized work and sloppy citation methods. This chapter ends with a section on APA style and format and provides useful information on how to avoid the most common writing errors and tips for improving all kinds of writing, not just scientific writing.

The literature review is often a key component of many types of scientific writing. You may be asked to write a stand-alone literature review, or a literature review might be part of a term paper or research paper. Chapter 5 provides guiding principles for writing literature reviews and also provides an actual sample from a former student of mine, including the first draft, an edited version, and the final draft. Seeing actual examples of the process will give you an insight into how to improve your own writing that few other books offer. If you will be writing a complete research paper, then chapter 6 is essential for you. In this chapter, I review each of the main sections of a research paper (Introduction, Method, Results, and Discussion), again including an actual student sample of each section's rough draft, edited version, and final version. In this way, you can see how instructors identify writing problems, and you can also see student solutions. By modeling this entire process for you, I show you how psychologists write and think, and, I hope, you will start to internalize and gain those abilities yourself. Chapter 7 outlines the remaining details of the research paper, including the title page, abstract, references, and tables. In my usual format, I provide examples of each so you can see actual student work.

Although the type of writing you would do for an undergraduate course in psychology is the major focus of this book, scientists also write for other reasons, and chapter 8 presents examples of other types of scientific writing. An essential component of being a good scientist is the ability to communicate to the larger scientific community, and we often accomplish that goal by attending regional or national conferences. As a student, you too might have the opportunity to attend or present at one of these conferences, and thus chapter 8 opens with examples of writing for an oral presentation at a conference and also provides an example of writing for a poster presentation at a conference. However, scientific information is also communicated in other ways, such as writing for the World Wide Web, and in this section I provide some ideas on how to tailor your scientific writing to take advantage of a Web presence, maximizing your format to how those using the Internet read and comprehend Web pages. During your college career, you may also be asked to write in the form of an essay exam, and I provide some tips on how to improve your writing for such exams. Finally, I close by discussing writing for both pleasure and insight. A number of medical studies have demonstrated the beneficial effects of writing for individuals with particular problems, such as fibromyalgia, breast cancer, and arthritis.

Of course, because it is your book, you can read the chapters in any order, but if you are actually conducting research for a psychology paper, I suggest you read chapters 2 and 3 before you start the actual writing of your research paper. If you are writing a term paper that is mostly your opinion, I would suggest chapters 1 and 4. If you are in a course such as research methods or experimental design, then I would recommend that you read all the chapters in order so you can see the process from start to finish. You will note that in many places I have used information from the Internet to provide cogent examples. In chapter 3, I present a section titled "Evaluating Sources," and I have followed the advice I present there in my selection of materials from the Internet. As I have been, always be careful about referencing information from the Internet, and ensure that the information and its source are credible and reliable.

It is my sincere hope that the ideas in the book will help you with your scientific writing. If you can think of anything that I can do to improve this book, please e-mail me at elandru@boisestate.edu. Your suggestions are both welcome and valuable, and in future editions of this book I will be able to add resources to improve my advice to undergraduate psychology students.

Why Psychology Students (and Not Just English Majors) Have to Write

1

> Give me a dozen healthy infants, well formed, and my own specified world to bring them up in, and I'll guarantee to take any one at random and train him to become any type of specialist I might select—doctor, lawyer, artist, merchant, chief, and, yes, even beggarman and thief, regardless of his talents, penchants, tendencies, abilities, vocations, and race of his ancestors
>
> —*John B. Watson,* Behaviorism

Have you ever tried to read an article in a scholarly journal and discovered that you understood very little of it? Scientific writers in psychology are often victimized by poor writing habits; as one author put it, they exert "a corrupting influence on young scientists—on their writing, their reading, and their thinking" (Woodford, 1967, as cited in Van Wagenen, 1991, pp. 2–3). As an undergraduate student, you are in a position right now to recognize these corrupting influences and put an end to poor scientific writing! Scientific writing need not be dull or boring, as you can see from this chapter's opening quotation. For a lab report, your professor may require a slightly more cautious tone than John B. Watson (1925) uses in this excerpt from his book *Behaviorism*, but then, part of becoming a good scientific writer is learning that how you want to present your message—be it in a scholarly article, popular book, public information Web site, or convention speech—affects the level of formality you use.

Scientific writing in psychology can be a difficult task because of its complexity. Like other complex skills, writing improves with practice, instruction, and feedback. Although writing scientifically for psychology requires some specialized skills, it also shares important characteristics with other types of writing with which you may already be familiar. The goal of this book is to help you become more confident in your ability to write scientifically.

There are different approaches to categorizing writing assignments, and it is important to note that scientific writing is not the "best" type of writing or the most valuable type of writing, but just one method of writing that attempts to achieve specific goals. One classification system suggests six major types of writing: expressive, exploratory, informative, scientific, literary, and persuasive (University of Maryland University College, 2005a). Even though we place our lab reports, literature reviews, term papers, and research papers into the "scientific writing" category, remember that scientific writing shares characteristics with other types of writing. Scientific writers are expressive, exploring topics in new and different ways, working to inform the reader, clearly placing the topic in a literary context, and persuading the reader to accept the results as presented. Thus, scientific writing is not an independent form of writing exclusive to other approaches, but may perhaps be thought of as an approach to writing in a particular style, following specific rules, and telling a story in an objective yet definitive voice. One way to build your confidence in your own scientific writing is to think of scientific writing as just one of several possible ways to approach telling a story.

Telling a Good Story With Scientific Information: Can It Be Done?

Even though it may not seem so in the psychological materials you read (textbooks, journal articles, Web sites, book chapters, etc.) and write (lab reports, literature reviews, term papers, research papers), good scientific writing tells a story. This idea of storytelling, even in scientific writing for psychology, is not new (e.g., Roediger, 2007; Salovey, 2000; Silvia, 2007; Trochim, 2001). However, not all scientific writers achieve the goal of good storytelling, as you can attest when you read a journal article and come away with no idea what it was about. The characteristics of good storytelling in literature also apply to good storytelling in scientific writing. For instance, much of the advice that Ballon (2005) gives to screenwriters also applies to scientific writers. In writing a screenplay, Ballon advises the writer, for example, to start with a topic or issue, relate the beginning to the ending, and hook the audience. Screenwriters are taught to develop a conflict and flesh out the relationship between protagonist (hero) and antagonist (villain). Scientific writing does the same, but not so dramatically. In testing the relationships between independent and dependent variables, other forces such as nuisance variables or confounds (antagonists) come into play that threaten the veracity of our conclusions. Screenwriters are also taught to write in a three-act structure, with Act I as the exposition, Act II as the complications, and Act III as the resolution (Ballon, 2005). Scientific writing follows a similar storytelling sequence, although the areas of emphasis for screenwriters and scientific writers are different. Screenwriters even have their own script format that must be followed, with formatting and layout rules and specialized terminology, like a slugline (the instruction written in the script as to the setting for the screenplay's action, and it is written in capital letters). Scientific writers also have specific rules to follow in the presentation of new scientific information. Good writing tells a compelling story, whether it be a screenplay or scientific journal article.

A similar analysis of the elements of storytelling is offered by Appelcline (n.d.). She lists these five tools of good storytelling: setting, character, plot, backstory, and detail. Interestingly, this summary of the elements of storytelling comes from an undergraduate student discussing online gaming (sometimes, a story is a story is a story!) The elements of storytelling are somewhat universal, and each of these elements is an important component of scientific writing in psychology. First, the character: What is the story about? Have you ever walked out of a movie theater confused about what the movie was about? The main character of the story must be clearly defined, or else we have problems following the story. In scientific writing, the "who" or the "character" may not be a person, but a behavioral variable or phenomenon of interest. The main character may be the effects of depression or studying the variables that predict career satisfaction. But if the variables are not clearly defined or the hypotheses are not carefully stated, we may have trouble following what the scientific story is all about.

Second, the backstory: What happened in the past that leads us to the present? Screenwriters and storytellers are quite adept at "filling in the blanks" and providing context for us to understand the story's dynamics and how the conflict unfolds and how that conflict is ultimately resolved. Scientific writing highly values the backstory, as seen in stand-alone literature reviews or literature reviews contained in term papers or research papers. The backstory is important in scientific writing because it provides the context of why one would bother to study a particular psychological phenomenon. And the backstory helps tell scientists what we already know, so we can focus on studying what we don't know.

Third, the plot: What is happening now? For the screenwriter, this would be Act II, or the complications. But for scientific writing, this differs. In scientific writing, the plot is revealed by the sequence of items presented to the reader. Background information is followed by current events, which are followed by outcomes and then interpretation of outcomes. Scientific writing describes what happened in the past, what is happening now, and what might happen in the future. As you can see, scientific writing is very linear and does not use common dramatic storytelling conventions, like flashbacks or foreshadowing. But any good story needs a good plot, otherwise the reader has a hard time caring about the story.

Fourth, the setting: Where is the story happening? In a good story, place, time, weather conditions, and other elements of the setting make it possible for readers to experience the narrative. Sometimes elements of the setting serve to move the action forward. Scientific writers use the Method section of their journal article or lab report to show where and how an experiment happened. If it seems relevant, they may tell more about the setting, such as the time the experiment took place, the conditions in the room, the instructions given to participants, and so forth. Scientists want to get a clear idea of the setting so they can understand the context in which a particular process took place and particular results were obtained—this is extremely helpful if the other scientists want to replicate (repeat) the study.

Fifth, the details: What specific items should the audience notice? Screenwriters and storytellers have numerous tools available to them to communicate to the audience, and with time and experience, they learn which are the most effective in a particular situation. The more you write scientifically, the more experience and confidence you will build. Scientific writing in psychology is very detail oriented in what it requires to be provided to the reader. The *Publication Manual of the American Psychological Association* (APA, 2010) prescribes many of the requirements that scientific writers must satisfy. Much of this book is devoted to helping you become a better scientific storyteller, and sometimes students feel at odds with this goal when constrained by the conventions of "APA style and format." However, having a preordained format may be more of a benefit than you think. Silvia (2007) describes it this way:

> Writing a journal article is like writing a screenplay for a romantic comedy: You need to learn a formula. As odd as it sounds, you should be grateful for APA style. Once you learn what goes where—and what never goes where—you'll find it easy to write journal articles. (pp. 78–79)

Silvia's advice applies to many types of scientific writing you'll be doing as an undergraduate psychology student.

Why Do We Tell the Scientific Story?

Clear communication using the elements of storytelling allows the writer to create a story in such a way that it will be memorable to others. Ultimately, the most important reason for scientific writing in psychology is for communication to others. The primary audience is usually professional psychologists or psychology students, but not always.

Many areas of psychology are indeed quite complex, but if readers with at least some technical knowledge of psychology have difficulty comprehending at least some aspect of a scientific writing in psychology, then the author has failed in his or her goal to communicate. But sometimes scientific writers have other motivations ("How Experts Communicate," 2000). Sometimes psychologists write to impress other psychologists. Unfortunately, some scientists have a tendency to equate plain language with oversimplification. Sometimes psychologists write in the same manner they were taught in graduate school, following the examples of their mentors. Sometimes psychologists write to obtain promotion and tenure. Although the goal of scientific writing should be the clear communication of ideas, in reality scientific writing is often sidetracked by goals that do not always promote clarity.

There is nothing wrong with scientific writing serving multiple goals, as long as clear communication is the utmost goal. There are many other motivations for writing. For instance, Gottschalk and Hjortshoj (2004) remind us of the various types of informal writing, especially student writing. Writing can be used to inform teachers, to learn, and to prepare for performance (see also Miller & Lance, 2006). Teachers use writing assignments such as the use of beginning-of-semester questionnaires, written evaluations, and 1-minute papers to obtain students' feedback on teacher performance. Teachers also use writing to help students learn by having them write reflection journals, participate in e-mail discussions, and answer study guide questions. Teachers also use writing to help students show what they know, for example, by using a rough draft–revised draft process in which students begin to understand the importance of a first draft in leading to a desirable final result.

Types of Assignments

Even within scientific writing for psychology, there exist myriad types of writing assignments. Miller and Lance (2006), in a review of the literature, identified 12 different types of writing assignments used in psychology: progressive papers, multiperspective papers, group papers, reflective writing, portfolios, interpretative writing, short writing, literature reviews, written feedback, reaction papers, knowledge maps, and student newspapers. Although I do not provide detailed instruction about each of these types of assignments, the basic ideas of style and editing and construction will provide helpful assistance for many, if not most, of these writing assignments. This book, however, focuses more closely on two of the most common (and perhaps most difficult) types of scientific writing in psychology: literature reviews and research papers. Whereas different types of scientific writing are briefly previewed here, in later chapters I delve more deeply into the mechanics of assignments, with examples, and demonstrate the writing techniques that can lead to success.

LAB REPORT

At many colleges and universities nationwide, laboratory (lab) sections accompany the coursework in a particular area. In psychology, you might encounter a course in cognitive psychology or physiological psychology that has an associated lab section in which students conduct mini-experiments during the lab and are asked to write lab reports as a method of summarizing the session's results. For example, in a lab associated with a human memory course, students may be asked to "experiment" on themselves and collect data based on the phenomenon being studied. An instructor could present students with a series of words based on the Stroop effect. Students are asked to say the color of the ink, not the word (but the words are actually color names), and the experimenter records how much time elapses and the number of errors (both dependent variables). Students in the class would then be asked to prepare a laboratory report. One benefit of the lab report is that it allows the instructor to determine the extent to which the student understands the hands-on exercise in the lab.

Entire books are devoted to the development of research skills using a laboratory approach in psychology (Crawford & Christensen, 1995; Langston, 2002). However, most lab reports are actually miniature versions of a complete research paper (Kennedy, n.d.; University of Richmond, 2010). Thus, the sections of a research paper—title page, abstract, introduction, Method, Results, Discussion, references, and tables or figures (if necessary)—would most likely be the sections of your lab report, only in a condensed version. You may find that your instructor wants a modified version of the above, with sections such as title, purpose, materials, procedure, observations and data, analysis of data, and conclusions (McConnell, 2000).

LITERATURE REVIEW

In some cases, a literature review might share some of the components of a lab report, but it is also often part of the first section of a term paper or research paper. The *literature* is a fairly generic term that can be used in a number of contexts. First, a student could write just a review of the literature. This would entail an integrated synopsis or summary of some aspect of the psychological literature related to a variable or behavior of interest. In addition, the literature review is often a key component of the "Introduction" portion of a research paper or lab report. Furthermore, depending on the type of term paper assignment, a review of the literature could be a key part of a term paper. Simply put, a literature review is a review of materials available on a particular topic, examining the most relevant, recent, and scholarly work in an area (Kemlo & Morgan, 2004).

Literature reviews are usually organized around a conflict or controversy, presenting both sides by reading and organizing all the relevant studies in a coherent manner, or by selecting just one point of view and selecting those studies that support your point (University of Washington, 2005). A literature review is not just a summary of articles or journals that you have read (Kemlo & Morgan, 2004), but an integrated resource that both analyzes and synthesizes the literature into a coherent and clear current status report. A well-written literature review is valuable to the reader because it presents a comprehensive view of previous work, providing a context for present and future work. This may be why components of literature review strategies are found in many types of scientific writing, including lab reports, term papers, and research papers. In fact, sometimes literature reviews are published as stand-alone text, called *review articles* (University of Washington, 2005).

Writing a literature review involves (a) formulating the problem or topic to be examined, (b) searching the available literature for relevant and topical work, (c) evaluating the literature and its appropriate contribution to providing a context to previous work, and (d) analyzing and interpreting the pertinent literature (Lyons, 2005). A well-written literature review is useful because it integrates the research of others; identifies similarities, differences, and trends in previous research; demonstrates a comprehensive knowledge of the topic; and exemplifies analysis and synthesis skills in the evaluation of reviewed materials. Because of the academic benefit of literature reviews, it is not a surprise that literature reviews are frequent components of writing assignments.

TERM PAPER

To be honest, *term paper* is such a generic phrase that it is difficult to summarize an exhaustive set of rules for every term paper. A term paper could be almost any type of assignment, including a reaction paper, a semester-long journal, an opinion paper, an argument–debate paper, and so on (Miller & Lance, 2006). Perhaps what distinguishes a term paper from other papers is that (a) it is prepared outside of class and (b) it is whatever your instructor says it is. In this context, I'll refer to a term paper as a nonexperimental research paper, that is, a paper in which original research is not being reported, for example, a summary of others' research findings. Typically, your instructor would assign a term paper to (a) help increase your expertise in a particular subject area and (b) help sharpen your analytic (critical thinking) and writing skills (McGraw-Hill/Dushkin, n.d.). Writing improvement takes practice, and term paper assignments help provide that practice, as well as giving the instructor some insight into your level of understanding of a particular subject or topic.

Because term papers are such a versatile writing assignment, they are used widely, but the requirements by discipline (and even within the same discipline) may also be widely different. Be sure to clarify key issues with your instructor, such as desired length, use of APA format, overall goals of the assignment, references versus works cited versus bibliography, and so forth.

RESEARCH PAPER

The research paper is where the details of an experiment are presented formally. One of the reasons why experimental research papers are so important in psychology is that they model the thinking processes that psychologists use. That is, as effective storytellers, we provide a character (topic to be studied), backstory (literature review), plot (hypotheses to be tested), setting (where and how the experiment was conducted), and detail (participants, materials, and procedure). Research papers resolve the preexisting conflicts between the previous literature and the current findings at the end of the paper, just as the screenwriter resolves plot conflicts in Act III. Research paper assignments, like most academic writing assignments, share the goals of teaching students a way of reading (like a psychologist) and a way of writing (like a psychologist; McCormick, 1994).

Meeting Audience Needs: What Is the Instructor Asking for?

Even though an instructor may have multiple goals for a writing assignment, to be successful in your scientific writing as a college student you must ultimately remember this: Give the instructor what he or she wants, or as Sternberg (2005) said more eloquently, write for your reader.

**Writing Maxim: Write for Your Audience
(Or, Give Your Instructor Exactly What He or She Wants)**

This means that you should completely understand the nature of the writing assignment before beginning writing. Although an instructor may say to prepare your assignment using APA format, does he or she mean all the rules (strict adherence) or most of the rules (less strict adherence)? It is essential that you ask the instructor what he or she wants in any type of writing assignment, or else you risk investing a great deal of effort into a writing assignment that may not turn out the way you expect. However, be careful not to become too cynical—sometimes this is a fine line to tread. For some instructors, you may have to play the game and pretty much give them what they want; but for other instructors, you'll explore your world of ideas and practice expressing those ideas scientifically. Perhaps the corollary to the writing maxim should be "Know Your Instructor."

This also means, however, that instructors need to be clear in communicating their expectations to students! You might ask your instructor whether he or she has a grading rubric available for your review (see my example in chapter 4). Sometimes, even when the instructor says "Write in APA format," it may not be as simple as that. For example, when I give the Introduction/Literature Review assignment in my Research Methods class, I like my students to spell out all the authors the first time a reference is mentioned, even if there are six or more authors. However, this directly contradicts APA style, which states that if there are six or more authors, you can use just the first author's name and *et al.* on the first use in the paper (e.g., "Landrum et al., 2005"). Why do I deviate from APA format? Because I think it is important to acknowledge the work of all the authors, not just the first. What if I were the sixth author—wouldn't I want my name mentioned? The *Publication Manual* (APA, 2010) recommends one or two spaces after a period at the end of a sentence; I prefer two spaces. Why? I think those sentences are easier for me to read, with more separation between them. The moral of the story is this: Even though an instructor might tell you he or she wants term papers prepared in APA format, be savvy enough to ask whether he or she has any personal preferences or exceptions that might not be apparent.

Sternberg (2005) offers four suggestions in achieving the goal of writing for your reader. First, make sure you use a vocabulary appropriate for the reader. Even though you may be writing for your college professors, you may be presenting a topic to them outside of their own expertise. If you find yourself using highly specialized terminology, be sure to either define it or present it in a context in which the definition can be understood. In other words, "eschew obfuscation." This advice comes from legendary editor and Furman University professor Dr. Charles Brewer, who often gave this advice to faculty members submitting manuscripts to the journal *Teaching of Psychology*. "Eschew obfuscation" is a clever way of communicating the idea to avoid writing in a confusing manner, or to seek out clarity. Good scientific writing communicates clearly. Thus, it is better to say "write clearly" than "eschew obfuscation" because the goal is for the reader to understand your writing, and ideally understand your writing without frequent use of a dictionary.

Second, maintain the appropriate level of formality for the writing situation. Quickly writing a 1-minute paper at the end of class is much different from handing in a research paper you have worked on all semester. Scientific writing tends to have a high level of formality because of the objectivity desired in the message. Students sometimes slip into conversation mode in their writing, for example, "Now I'll talk about the process of synaptic transmission." Although a good scientific writer wants the reader to become engaged with the topic, scientific writing is not a conversation between writer and reader. But wait! Throughout this chapter (and throughout this book) I have been referring to *you* and *us*—that isn't APA format, is it? It is not! I am not writing this book in APA format, even though parts of this book are about APA format. Rather, I'm writing this book for you, in hopes of connecting with you and expressing my ideas about writing scientifically. I too must know my audience, and in this case, it is not a journal reviewer, but you.

Third, include only those details that are relevant to your audience. When writing for your instructor, you will probably not need to define terms like *independent variable* and *dependent variable*, but you might have to define such terms if you were writing for a broader audience, such as the general public.

Last, avoid abbreviations. Not only can they be distracting, but an editorial in *Nature Neuroscience* ("How Experts Communicate," 2000) makes the point that unfamiliar abbreviations make additional demands on memory and that "clear writing reduces the demands on working memory by presenting information where readers expect to find it" (p. 97). If you cannot avoid abbreviations, then try to use them sparingly, as the *Publication Manual* (APA, 2010) suggests. It states that to be worth the effort, the item being abbreviated should be used at least three times after introduction (and when introducing the item, always spell it out the first time unless the abbreviation is accepted as a word; see p. 107

of the *Publication Manual*). The key issue is this: Is the space saved by the abbreviation worth the effort by the reader to master the meaning of the abbreviation (APA, 2010)?

Why APA Style and Format Exist

In the early 20th century, there were only a handful of journals in the social sciences, and journal editors determined the shape and content of published works. As scholarship in the social sciences developed, the number of journals and articles in these disciplines proliferated. Inconsistency in reporting standards and in basic layout of content led to confusion among researchers and other authors and consumers of the scientific literature. A standard format began to appear in the 1890s, thanks to Joseph Jastrow at the University of Wisconsin (Blumenthal, 1991). As an alternative to long essays in early psychological journals, Jastrow suggested that "minor studies" be published by stating a problem, describing the research methods used, followed by the findings, data analysis, and a conclusion. Jastrow's imprint on scientific writing in psychology is still with us today.

In 1928, editors and business managers of psychological and anthropological journals met to discuss, among other things, the typical format and information that a published journal article should provide (up to that time, individual journal editors helped determine the shape and content of published works). In a 6½ page article published in *Psychological Bulletin* in 1929, Bentley et al. provided suggestions to authors to guide their preparation of manuscripts. This guidance was organized into four main sections: (a) general form of manuscript, (b) subdivision and articulation of topics, (c) references and footnotes, and (d) tabular matter and illustrations. These guidelines were revised again in 1944, but expanded to 32 pages of advice, and the first *Publication Manual* was published (as a separate volume, not appearing in *Psychological Bulletin*) in 1952 (Roediger, 2004).

Subsequent editions of the *Publication Manual* included more detail, which added to its page length as well; the sixth edition (APA, 2010) is 272 pages long. Some writers have suggested that the *Publication Manual* is overly prescriptive and rule based (Roediger, 2004; Vipond, 1993). The *Publication Manual* is indeed more of a guide to a style of scientific writing than only a specification of the format in which to present scientific information, and this style and format is used not only in psychology but in a host of other disciplines, including social work, education, nursing, business, and coaching.

Reading a paper prepared in accordance with APA format may not be overly entertaining, but the linear presentation of ideas and events enhances the objectivity and formality that science ascribes to. Although research is not always conducted in a linear fashion, there is a linearity to the general thought process. Generally, a scientist comes up with an idea and researches the background of that idea, yielding testable hypotheses. He or she then conducts a study to test those hypotheses, followed by analyses to determine whether the hypotheses were supported or refuted. The scientist then discusses the general meaning of his or her work, concluding with the limitations of the study and suggestions for future work. The linear thought process of the scientist is reflected in the linearity of APA format and the structure of scientific writing. When the work is written to be shared with others, it is framed in this linear sequence. Just like good storytelling, as discussed earlier in this chapter, understanding character development and backstory provides a context in which to appreciate the plot and the resolution of the character conflict. Scientific writing provides the same backstory and character development so that the plot can be resolved, but the plot centers on psychological ideas and behaviors rather than people.

This linearity of presentation may seem boring to some, but after some experience in reading psychological literature, you come to expect the sequence and appreciate it. It provides a structure and framework common to scientific thinking and work and makes sense to scientists. Have you ever watched a movie in which the storyline is presented out of sequence? Some movies like to use flashbacks as a creative device to assist in dramatic storytelling. When flashbacks are used too much, it becomes hard to follow the story and make sense of what is happening. I find myself thinking "Is this now or then?" rather than fully comprehending the story. As scientists, we aspire to not let the structure and framework of the story detract from the story itself.

Later portions of this book delve more deeply into the details of APA format for our different types of writing assignment. In fact, although I refer to the rules of writing as APA format, APA refers to a style of writing, as presented at http://www.apastyle.org. Vipond (1993) refers to this APA style of scientific writing as *plain style* and suggests three main elements of plain style: clarity, literal writing, and brevity. Writing in a clear and orderly style promotes clarity, which is also associated with logical and smooth writing. *Literal writing* prefers a straightforward approach to the presentation of ideas while avoiding a creative approach to writing, such as the use of literary devices (e.g., alliteration, rhyming, poetic expressions, and clichés). Finally, brevity (or *economy of expression*, as in the sixth edition of the *Publication Manual*) is highly valued, as in "say only what needs to be said" (APA, 2010, p. 67).

Writing a research paper is a complex task, and a number of resources exist, such as Web sites (e.g., Plonsky, 2006) and books (e.g., Mitchell,

Jolley, & O'Shea, 2004; Szuchman, 2005). However, the ultimate guide for the preparation of research papers in psychology is the *Publication Manual*. Many of the guides available for writing research papers help to interpret the complex APA style and formatting rules, and this book also provides concrete examples of how to navigate through the complexity of APA format. But before starting your first scientific writing assignment, there is much work to be done—we need a foundation on which to build. Both planning and researching are essential foundational components to successful scientific writing, and we turn to these next.

Starting Your Paper: Finding the Thread of Your Story

2

> I have a vast deal to say, and shall give all this morning to my pen. As to my plan of writing every evening the adventures of the day, I find it impracticable; for the diversions here are so very late, that if I begin my letters after them, I could not go to bed at all.
>
> —*Frances Burney*, Evelina

Although in a different context, this author sounds just as busy as today's college student. There are so many different demands on students that finding the time to complete writing assignments is hard enough; thus, this chapter is about the planning processes that should precede your scientific writing in psychology. Although assignments may differ widely, these suggestions will help organize your thoughts and your approach to the writing assignment, making the assignment easier to complete and facilitating earning a better grade.

Selecting a Topic

For some assignments, you'll be provided with a topic by your instructor. For others, you'll be given a range of topics to write about, and sometimes the topic can be nearly anything. Before you start writing, even before you start researching, you need to seriously consider your topic, and plan out how you will treat that topic in your paper. The plan may be very brief, such as for an opinion paper, or it may be fixed, such as for lab report. By *plan*, I don't necessarily mean a complete outline, although outlines can be extremely helpful. Planning in this context means not only selecting a topic, but also knowing where you are going, including the goals of your writing. Your writing goal could simply be the clear communication of ideas (although this is not so simple), writing to demonstrate to teachers what you know, writing to learn, or writing in preparation for performance (such as rough drafts). In the last chapter of this book, I'll address other types of writing, too.

Obviously, you will want to select a topic that will allow you to successfully satisfy the instructor's goals for the writing assignment. When students are given a wide range of possible topics, the level of "freedom" is sometime daunting because you might be torn between writing about what you want to write about versus writing about what you think your instructor wants you to write about. If you are unsure, ask the instructor in class or privately in an e-mail or during office hours. Odds are, if you are wondering about a question, someone else in the class has the same question, too! If the possible topic pool is broad, here are some ideas (modified from Landrum & Davis, 2007; Martin, 1991) on how to generate topics to write about, especially research topics.

OBSERVATION

Looking at the world around you may give you some great ideas to write about. Sometimes just sitting on a bench at the mall or in the park can present ideas about human behavior that could be fascinating to think about and write about. Given that I ride the elevator six floors up and down on a regular basis, I see all sorts of elevator behavior that would be fascinating to write about (yes, I know I should take the stairs more often). You can obtain good topics to write about just by carefully observing the world you live in.

VICARIOUS OBSERVATION

Perhaps someone told you about a situation or event they witnessed, and you found it hard to believe—this would be an example of vicarious observation. In reading your textbook for your psychology class, you read the author's account of a famous study and begin wondering whether those results would apply today. You can get good ideas from others' thoughts and observations as well as from your own.

EXPAND ON PREVIOUS IDEAS

Perhaps in an earlier class you wrote a literature review on a particular topic but did not have the opportunity to conduct the study—that could be a source of a topic to write about. Or you may have heard an instructor hypothesize about a "what-if" situation, but you were hard pressed to believe the hypothesis. Previous ideas are a good source of writing topics. You may have had an interest in a topic for some time but never had the chance to explore it while in college—expanding on your own previous ideas can also be a good source of topics.

FOCUS ON A PRACTICAL PROBLEM

I often suggest that students pick a topic to write about that, if they had all the time in the world, they would write about anyway. In other words, try to find a topic that can help you answer a real question that you have—completing the assignment and doing the writing are much more pleasurable when you are studying something of personal interest. I once had a student ask me about the impact of withdrawals ("Ws") on her transcript because she was thinking of applying to graduate school. I didn't know the answer, so that became a great topic for us to study (Montoya, Smit, & Landrum, 2000) and resulted in a published research paper (Landrum, 2003).

These are just some of the ways in which you might think about selecting a topic to write about, especially if the topic is not determined for you by your instructor. Although I've outlined some good sources for getting ideas, Sternberg (2005) lists a number of mistakes that students can make when selecting a topic, including (a) selecting a topic that is not interesting to them, (b) selecting a topic too easy or too safe, (c) selecting a topic that is too difficult, (d) selecting a topic with inadequate literature available, and (e) selecting a topic that is too broad. In some cases, you may not have enough autonomy to select your own topic, so you may or may not be interested in what you write about. However, if you do have the opportunity to choose a topic, choose one in which you have an intrinsic interest. Sometimes students select a topic that is too easy or too safe, such as writing about a topic they have already written about in another class. If you think about doing this, be sure to check with your instructor to see whether this is OK—in some cases, you may be accused of plagiarizing or cheating if you "double dip," or use one paper for two different purposes (I'll clarify this later in chapter 4 in the section on plagiarism).

Another benefit of planning is the ability to give yourself an adequate amount of time to complete the assignment with the best chances of success. This means you should always quickly peruse the literature, including what is available at your library, before committing to a writing topic. Although you want to write about a challenging topic, and learn about the topic in the process, you do not want to choose something too difficult. If it is a particular subspecialty in psychology, the vocabulary may be too steep to learn in time to write a coherent paper. Selecting a topic with inadequate literature could mean that very little has been published on the topic, or it could mean that little literature will be available to you in the time you have to complete the assignment. Your library can certainly order journal articles and books for you, but depending on their availability, you may not be able to access them in time to complete your assignment.

Finally, sometimes students select a topic that is much too broad, such as "children with depression." This topic is much too broad for a lab report, term paper, or research paper and would require a literature review of volumes and volumes. In later chapters, I'll present more ideas on how to narrow your topic appropriately, but don't forget your most valuable resource of all in topic selection—your instructor! Your instructor wants to read a good paper and wants you to learn from the writing assignment, so he or she is motivated to help you get off to a good start by selecting an appropriate topic. Once the topic has been determined, the next step (depending on the assignment) may be to formulate either a thesis statement or a research question.

Developing a Thesis Statement or a Research Question

You may be familiar with the term *thesis statement* from a previous English composition course. In fact, some of your psychology faculty may direct you to write a term paper using a thesis statement (although a thesis statement would be used much less frequently in a lab report or research paper). See Table 2.1 for examples of thesis statements. The thesis of your paper is the topic that you are writing about, plus a specific assertion about that topic (Online Writing Laboratory, 2004). Brunsvold (2003) offers a more complete description of what a thesis statement is, and what it is not. A thesis statement

- is an assertion, not a statement of fact;
- takes a stand, rather than introducing a topic;
- is a main idea, not a title;
- is narrow rather than broad, and is specific rather than general; and
- makes one main point rather than several main points (several main points may be difficult for the reader to follow).

Brunsvold suggests that a thesis statement be a complete sentence explaining, in some detail, the topic you are writing about. Following our maxim, if your instructor requests a thesis statement, be sure to provide it in the format and manner requested.

In a more typical type of psychology writing assignment, you may be asked to provide a research question rather than a thesis statement.

TABLE 2.1

Thesis Statement Examples

Not so good	Better
It is a fact that individuals who are more liberal do a better job recycling.	The degree to which a person chooses to recycle may be related to his or her political beliefs.
Researchers who rely on survey methodology are unaware of the disadvantages of response rate, lack of anonymity, and cost per respondent.	Survey outcomes need to be considered in the context of the limitations of survey research methodology.
Homelessness is unfair to children.	Children who are homeless are at risk to experience multiple deficits in their cognitive development.
The effect of student study time on classroom performance.	The effectiveness of student study strategies is influenced by more than time on task.

A good research question may be critical to your success for scientific writing in psychology. A coherent and well-formed research question will help guide the rest of the research process, helping you to determine what information is relevant to your writing assignment and what information is not. Depending on the type of writing assignment, your research question will be essential if you are developing testable hypotheses, such as for a research paper or research proposal.

Some of the characteristics of a superior thesis statement also apply to the development of a research question. For instance, your research question should not be too broad, but it should also not be so narrow that the research is not "do-able" within the constraints of the assignment or the task. The examples in Table 2.2 show a balance between what is too broad and too narrow in creating a research question.

After you have formulated your thesis statement or research question, evaluate it (Empire State College, n.d.-a). Put another way, ask the "so-what" question (Danya International, 2003). Let's say your paper topic is about recycling. If you were to ask yourself the so-what question, you would ask "So what about recycling?" You should be able to provide a compelling answer to why recycling is important, and why writing a paper or doing research about recycling is also important. Ask your instructor whether he or she cares about your topic, or whether his or her response is "So what?" More important, ask yourself the so-what question. If you have control over the topic you write about, try to select a topic you are passionate about and have an intrinsic interest in so that you can answer the so-what question with ease. For instance, if you have just been told that one of your grandparents has Parkinson's disease, you might choose to do your paper about that topic. If you can

TABLE 2.2

Research Question Examples

Too broad	Good balance	Too narrow
Why do adolescents smoke?	What is the impact of peer smoking on an adolescent's decision to smoke or not?	If an adolescent's parents are divorced (one parent has remarried and one parent has not), and if one of those parents smoke, does the adolescent begin smoking?
Does marriage make a person happy?	What is the relationship between age at marriage, marriage longevity, and marital satisfaction?	What is the best combination of exact ages for two people to be married and also be happy for most of the marriage?
How can students improve test scores?	What is the association between cumulative student study effort and test performance?	If a student studies 2 hours before the test, and another 2 hours the day before the test, will the student perform well?

write about topics you are already interested in, it becomes a "two-for-one" special—you satisfy the requirements of the assignment and you learn about something you were interested in anyway.

If the answer to your so-what question is "Nobody cares anyway," try to find another way to spin your topic into a more timely thesis statement or research question. If your thesis statement is "Parkinson's disease causes a lot of pain to many individuals," it is difficult to get excited about because it is so dry. However, "One in every 272 Americans suffers from the multiple debilitating effects of Parkinson's disease, affecting not only the afflicted individuals but also countless numbers of family members" is much more persuasive and compelling. Sometimes when students or colleagues ask me about the research I do, I tell a pretty convincing story about why the topic is important to me. In fact, if I cannot tell a good story, then I should think about why I am doing that research in the first place! If you are doing research, for a paper or as a research assistant, you too need to be able to persuasively tell your research story to others. Being able to tell a compelling and persuasive story can be helpful to your future in a number ways, ranging from self-confidence in a job interview, to competence in an area important for success in graduate school applications, or even to applying for undergraduate grants to do research. When departments hire faculty members, they ask prospective faculty about their program of research—and prospective faculty should be excited about it and able to communicate it clearly. When you go home for your holiday break and someone asks about your research paper, you too should be able to describe your work in a compelling fashion.

Uncovering the Backstory, Part 1: Your Library Search Strategy

The final part of this chapter presents some general thoughts about your strategy to find supporting information for your scientific writing assignment. I'll present specific details in the next chapter, but here I'll present some ideas about how to organize and plan your search strategy before you implement it.

PsycINFO is an incredibly useful database for beginning research on almost every topic possible in psychology. PsycINFO is published by the American Psychological Association (APA), and it is offered through a number of vendors. You will need to look into the database collection at your college or university library to see whether you have access to PsycINFO. As of November 2007, the PsycINFO database contained more than 3 million records, covering more than 2,400 journal titles (APA, 2012c). For current information on PsycINFO coverage, please visit the APA Web site at http://www.apa.org/pubs/databases/psycinfo/index.aspx. If you are searching for psychological literature, including journals, books, or even dissertations, PsycINFO is most likely the best place to start. In fact, the reference materials cataloged in PsycINFO range back to the early 1800s. Figure 2.1 shows what some PsycINFO search screens might look like. The look and feel of the system at your institution may be different, depending on the delivery platform your campus uses. However, depending on how the product is available on your campus, your screen might not look exactly like these.

As you can see, there are multiple options in conducting your PsycINFO search. Following are some factors for you to consider to help facilitate your search and to reduce the number of relevant articles ("hits") to a manageable number.

First, you'll have to make some decisions about your search terms. This is perhaps the most important step of the entire process! The database uses a specific vocabulary. For instance, if you were to search on the term *depression,* your search would have different results than if you searched on *depressing, depressive,* or even *depressed.* Thus, to search effectively, you have to know what you are doing. Sometimes the most

FIGURE 2.1

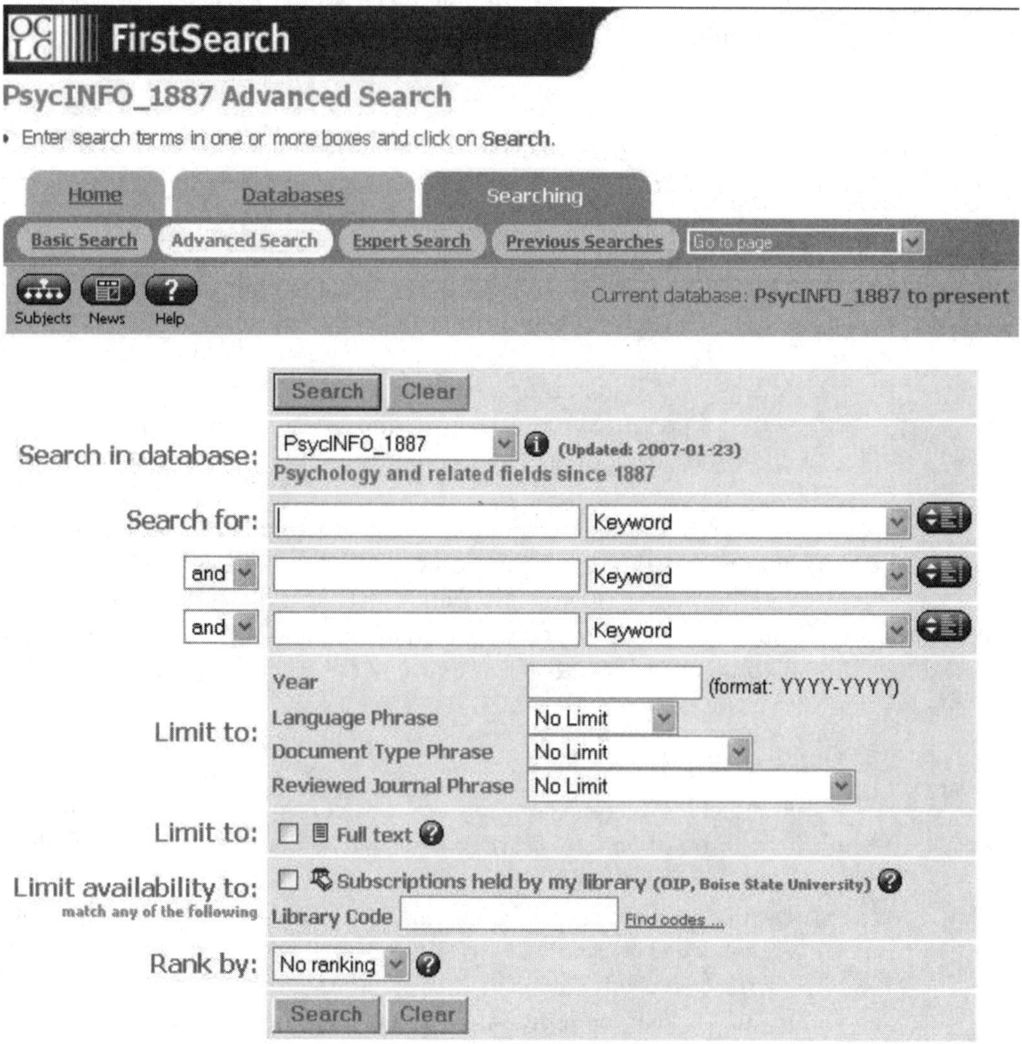

Example of PsycINFO search screens.

difficult decision is to determine what search term you should be using. For instance, if you were writing a term paper, would you search on *manic-depressive disorder* or *bipolar disorder?* The APA has published the *Thesaurus of Psychological Index Terms* (APA, 2007). This resource is devoted to helping researchers identify the correct terms for searching databases, and it offers very helpful suggestions for narrowing or broadening your search. A sample record with explanatory notes about the codes used in the print version of the thesaurus appears in Figure 2.2.

FIGURE 2.1 (*Continued*)

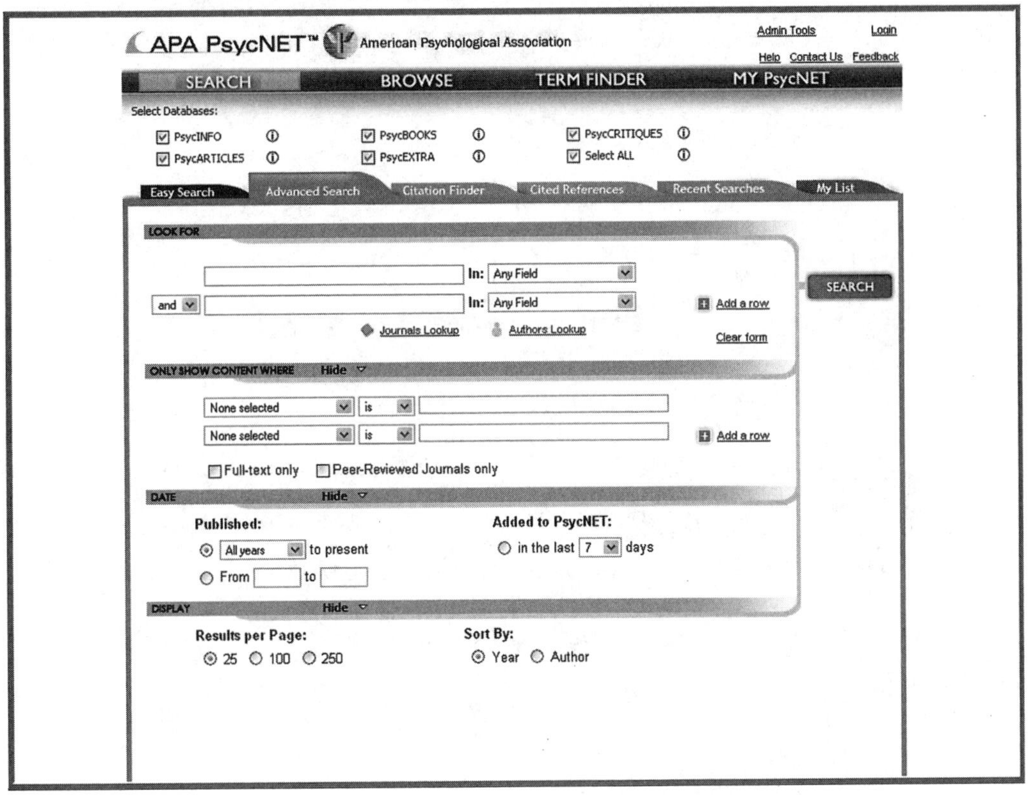

Example of PsycINFO search screens.

In addition to searching for keywords (which the thesaurus is invaluable in identifying), in PsycINFO you can also search on many other fields, such as author, title, and publisher, in addition to a keyword or index term search. An online thesaurus is available on all versions of PsycINFO. It is extremely useful because it enables you to see broader and narrower terms.

Another search feature in PsycINFO and many other databases is the use of Boolean operators, such as AND, NOT, and OR. For instance, conducting a keyword search on *depression* AND *children* will give you results with those keywords. Searching on *depression* OR *children* will broaden the search and return all the index entries referencing depression or referencing children, without necessarily overlapping. A search on *depression* NOT *children* will narrow your search, including records on the topic of depression but excluding those records that report *children* in the keywords. A different method of broadening the search is called *truncating*. In truncating, you allow the database to search for records

FIGURE 2.2

Anatomy of a Term
HOW TO READ A TERM RECORD

Postable Index Term (with date of entry)	**Peripheral Neuropathy** 2006
Posting Note and Subject Code Number of postings and unique five-digit code	**PN** 162 **SC** 37575
Scope Note Provides a definition and/or information about the proper use of the term	**SN** Disease or degenerative state of the peripheral nerves in which motor, sensory, or vasomotor nerve fibers may be affected.
Historical Note Provides information about the historical usage of a term since its introduction to the Thesaurus.	**HN** In May 2006, this term was created to replace the discontinued term PERIPHERAL NERVE DISORDERS. PERIPHERAL NERVE DISORDERS was removed from all records containing it and replaced with PERIPHERAL NEUROPATHY, its postable counterpart.
Used For (Non-postable term)	**UF** Peripheral Nerve Disorders
Broader Terms	**B** Nervous System Disorders 1967
Narrower Terms (Down arrow indicates more specific terms)	**N** ↓ Neuralgia 1973
Related Terms (Down arrow indicates more specific terms)	**R** Muscular Dystrophy 1973 ↓ Paralysis 1973 ↓ Peripheral Nervous System 1973

Sample term record. From *Thesaurus of Psychological Index Terms* by the American Psychological Association, 2007. Retrieved from http://www.apa.org/pubs/databases/training/thesaurus-intro.aspx. Copyright 2007 by the American Psychological Association.

that contain, in any form, the fragment of the keyword you provide. So, instead of searching on *depression* AND *depressing* AND *depressed* AND *depressive,* in truncating you would conduct a search for *depress**. The asterisk, called a *wildcard,* allows you to find any record that starts with *depress,* no matter how the word ends. This search would also find records you might not expect, such as records using the keyword *depresses.*

In addition to PsycINFO, there are many other places to find valuable psychological information. Table 2.3 provides some additional

TABLE 2.3

Examples of Online Resources

Name of database	Web site	What it covers
PsycARTICLES	http://www.apa.org/pubs/databases/psycarticles/index.aspx	Full-text compilation of APA published journals.
PsycINFO	http://www.apa.org/pubs/databases/psycinfo/index.aspx	Contains abstracts of published psychological literature.
ERIC (Educational Resources Information Center)	http://www.eric.ed.gov/	Provides abstracts of educational literature with full-text access via ERIC Document Reproduction Service.
MedlinePlus PubMed	Medlineplus.gov http://www.ncbi.nlm.nih.gov/PubMed/	Contains abstracts of articles from sources that publish biomedical research.
Sociological Abstracts	http://www.csa.com/factsheets/socioabs-set-c.php	Covers sociology and related disciplines in the behavioral and social sciences.
Social Sciences Citation Index	http://thomsonreuters.com/products_services/science/science_products/a-z/social_sciences_citation_index/	Multidisciplinary database that covers all of the social sciences and allows for citation searching.
Science Citation Index	http://thomsonreuters.com/products_services/science/science_products/a-z/science_citation_index/	Multidisciplinary database that covers the "hard" sciences and allows for citation searching.
SIRS Researcher (Social Issues Researcher)	http://www.proquestk12.com/productinfo/sirs_researcher.shtml	Contains full-text articles that explore social, scientific, health, historic, economic, business, political, and global issues.
PsycEXTRA	http://www.apa.org/pubs/databases/psycextra/index.aspx	Gray literature indexed from a psychological perspective. The file includes full-text documents for 70% of the records, including technical reports, position papers, conference presentations, and so on.
GrayLIT Network	http://www.osti.gov/graylit/	Comprehensive portal to federal gray literature; allows the user to find information without knowing the sponsoring agency.

(Continued)

TABLE 2.3 (*Continued*)

Examples of Online Resources

Name of database	Web site	What it covers
National Technical Information Service	http://www.ntis.gov/	Central resource for government-funded scientific, technical, engineering, and business-related information.
Virtual Technical Reports Center	http://www.lib.umd.edu/ ENGIN/TechReports/ Virtual-TechReports.html	Organizes institutions and provides links to technical reports, preprints, reprints, dissertations, theses, and research reports.
PsycBOOKS	http://www.apa.org/pubs/ databases/psycbooks/index. aspx	Provides access to APA books, out-of-print and classic texts. Includes an electronic version of the *Encyclopedia of Psychology*.
PsycCRITIQUES	http://www.apa.org/pubs/ databases/psyccritiques/ index.aspx	Extensive database of book reviews. Includes archive from *Contemporary Psychology: APA Review of Books*.

Note. This table was compiled in part by using resources from Kidd, Meyer, and Olesko (2000) and McCarthy and Pusateri (2006).

helpful resources that you may want to consult in addition to your PsycINFO search. Note that some of the Web sites below may only provide information about the database, not access to it. You should ask your instructor or a librarian for more information about what databases are available to you at your college or university.

For most scientific writing in psychology, PsycINFO is the best place to start. Its versatility allows for subject, keyword, and author searches, making it a very powerful tool. However, there is one other very powerful search tool that seems to be less known to students—the Social Sciences Citation Index (SSCI). Using SSCI's citation search feature, you can find out what authors have cited other authors from previous work. This is a powerful tool for following a line of research from an early, seminal article through to today. Let me give you an example. Say your assignment is to write a literature review on cognitive dissonance theory. You identify that the real start to this theory came in 1957 when Leon Festinger wrote *A Theory of Cognitive Dissonance* (you could have discovered this through a PsycINFO search, the instructor of your social psychology course, or even from the social psychology chapter of your introductory psychology textbook). The SSCI database will allow you to see who has cited Festinger (1957) since its publication. An example of what this type of output might look like is shown in Figure 2.3.

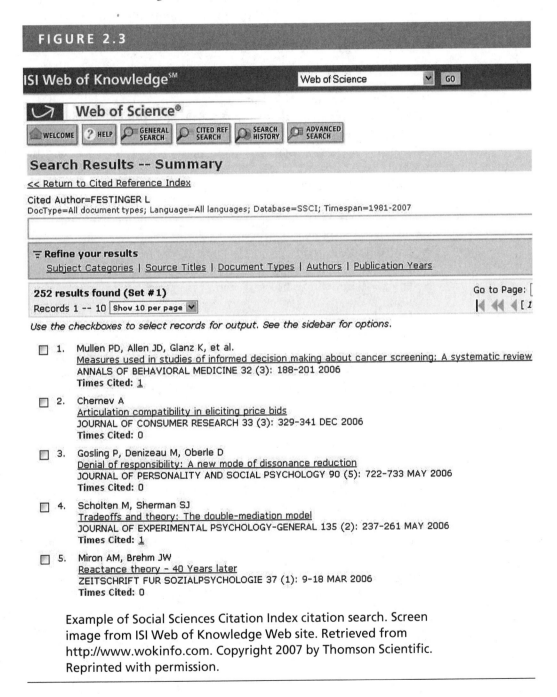

FIGURE 2.3

Example of Social Sciences Citation Index citation search. Screen image from ISI Web of Knowledge Web site. Retrieved from http://www.wokinfo.com. Copyright 2007 by Thomson Scientific. Reprinted with permission.

What Sources Are Allowed?

As part of the planning process, you should clarify with your instructor what sources are allowable, that is, what types of works can be cited. For instance, some amount of personal opinion may be appropriate in a term paper, but not in a research paper. Your instructor might want a literature review to be limited to published journal articles and books, not Internet sources. This is, however, more complicated than it may seem. Some journals now publish paper editions and also publish the work electronically on the Internet. Would it be allowable to cite the HTML version of an article that also appeared in print? If not, can you cite a scanned PDF version of the printed article? Is it allowable to cite an article that is published electronically ahead of print, by either the author or the publisher? How about an article that has been submitted for publication but not yet peer reviewed, or an article that is "in press" (accepted for publication but not yet published)? Is it allowable to cite auxiliary electronic content from an article when that content does not appear in the print edition? Be sure to clarify this before your research begins so that you won't waste time and effort.

You may also want to inquire about the relevance of popular sources versus more academic sources. Would it be appropriate to include information from magazines such as *Psychology Today, Omni, Reader's Digest,* or *Scientific American?* Do the articles you cite in your paper need to be peer reviewed? If you're looking for other sources of credible information, you may also want to explore PsycEXTRA, an APA database that covers materials disseminated outside of peer-reviewed journals. It includes technical reports and conference proceedings and other hard-to-find publications.

JOURNALS

How is a journal article different from a magazine article? Perhaps the fundamental difference between a magazine and a journal is how the article is published. Journals in psychology operate under a peer-review system in which manuscript submissions are reviewed by multiple referees before an acceptance decision is made. Let's say that you wanted to publish the results of your research in a psychology journal (and there are journals especially for psychology undergraduates—one example is the *Psi Chi Journal of Undergraduate Research*). After selecting which journal to send your manuscript to (not always an easy task), you would send multiple copies to its editor. Note that as a general rule, you may only submit a manuscript to one journal at a time. The editor sends copies of your manuscript out for review, which is where the peer-review process begins. Your peers in the field (other psychologists) are asked to review your manuscript and decide whether it is suitable for publication. These peers are also called *referees*, and you will sometimes hear the phrase "refereed journal" (which means the journal follows this peer-review process). Reviewers are often individuals with prior success in publishing their own manuscripts.

How does an individual reviewer evaluate a manuscript? Of course, this varies across journals and individuals, but in general, scholarship is the key. For the manuscript to be considered scholarly, there should be a thorough review of the literature, a keen grasp of the subject matter, concise writing, adequate research skills, demonstrated importance of the work to psychology, and an understanding of the journal readership (the journal subscribers).

Reviews are often done anonymously, that is, the writer is unaware of who the reviewers are. Sometimes, journal article submissions are masked—that is, the reviewers also do not know who the author is. Authors can request a masked review, and sometimes it is a journal's policy to mask review all submissions. This procedure is used in an effort to be as fair and objective as possible and to give full consideration to the contribution a journal article can make to the larger body of scientific knowledge.

MAGAZINES AND OTHER POPULAR SOURCES

The peer-review process required for journal publication differs from that of a magazine in that a magazine pays people to write articles. Authors of journal articles are not paid and are sometimes even asked to help defray the cost of journal publishing. Although magazine articles may be checked for accuracy, they do not undergo the scrutiny and examination that journal articles do. The majority of journal articles are well documented with supporting references noted as to when an idea has been borrowed from elsewhere. A magazine article is rarely as extensive in documenting the author's academic and scholarly work. One other minor difference between the two is that journals are typically not available for purchase at newsstands but must be subscribed to, whereas magazines are typically available at a newsstand or bookstore. In addition to magazines, there are, as you already know, numerous other outlets for information, including newspapers, television, radio, wikis, blogs, podcasts, and so forth. Remember to ask your instructor if you are unsure about what potential sources of information are allowable for your writing assignment.

GRAY LITERATURE

Gray literature refers to documents not commercially available (e.g., via a book or a journal) that may be of value but also may be difficult to authenticate and verify (Mathews, 2004). APA provides a gray literature database called PsycEXTRA, which includes documents such as research reports, policy statements, annual reports, standards, videos, conferences papers and abstracts, fact sheets, newsletters, pamphlets, directories, popular magazines, white papers, and grant information (APA, 2012b). You should know that items that appear in PsycEXTRA do not overlap with items available in PsycINFO and that PsycEXTRA is a fee-based service (you should check to see whether your library subscribes to PsycEXTRA, just as they subscribe to PsycINFO). You may be able to find many of the same items in PsycEXTRA with your own Internet search, but the benefit of PsycEXTRA is that it is organized, indexed, and updated every 2 weeks, and more than 70% of the items in PsycEXTRA have full-text links. But be careful—just because a PsycINFO or PsycEXTRA search result contains a full-text link does not mean that the article is of higher quality; it just means that it is more convenient for you to obtain. YOU still must determine whether the resource is relevant to your writing assignment.

Now you need to put your library search strategy into action. Once you start turning up resources that might be useful, you'll need to ask yourself, "Is this resource useful? How do I extract the most relevant information from each resource? How do I keep track of all the bits and pieces of information I am extracting from the literature?" The next chapter helps to answer these questions for you.

Extracting the Useful Nuggets From a Literature Search | 3

> Moreover, the most painstaking and laborious research,
> covering long periods of years, is necessary in order
> to accumulate the material for any history worth
> writing at all.
>
> *—Theodore Roosevelt,* History as Literature

This chapter aims to demystify the literature search and the processes of analyzing and synthesizing the research literature; however, it would be irresponsible of me to claim that these processes are anything short of painstaking and laborious, as noted in the quotation above. I hope you will find that by putting considerable time into a well-organized literature search, you will save time when it comes to composing the paper and will, I hope, earn a better grade. Scientific writing relies on the presentation of facts, theories, and hypotheses in an impartial and objective manner. Scientific writing generally strives to avoid the personal opinions of the writer and attempts to test the validity of ideas. A major component of this approach is the ability to incorporate evidence, specifically research-based evidence, into the written product. Chapter 2 ended with an organizational plan for finding relevant information for your scientific writing project; this chapter addresses implementing that search strategy, evaluating possible sources, and analyzing and extracting information from those sources.

Uncovering the Backstory, Part 2: Primary and Secondary Sources

An effective search strategy begins with the organizational foundation presented at the end of chapter 2. Knowing your keywords and exhausting relevant databases are important first steps. Next comes the actual research, evaluating sources, and extracting and analyzing information. You will, as much as possible, want to retrieve primary sources. What are primary sources? A primary source is an original document. For example, if you read a journal article about original research and the article was written by the researcher, that is a primary source. If you read about the original research, but what you read was not written by the original researcher but appeared in another journal article or a textbook, it would be a secondary source. Essentially, authors cannot control how others interpret their work—they can only control what they write. As scientists, we prefer primary sources whenever possible. This gives us the opportunity to understand the writer's perspective, as opposed to someone else's perspective.

In the last chapter, I detailed a number of databases from which you would typically obtain leads about the research available on the topic you are writing about (e.g., PsycINFO, ERIC, Social Sciences Citation Index). Here I highlight other resources and avenues you might pursue in implementing your search strategy.

ONLINE CATALOG

After you've conducted your database searches, you'll need to know what is available at your library. There should be an online search engine that will help you identify available resources (to obtain resources that are not available at your library, you may need to look into an interlibrary loan).

MAGAZINES

Magazines can often be a good source of ideas for topics to write about, and a magazine article may give you tips on primary sources to find. In general, however, you will typically not be citing magazine articles in scientific writing.

JOURNALS

Journals are often the preferred "currency" of scientific writing. Because of the rigorous standards of refereed journals, their credibility is highly valued. Journals are often preferred because of timeliness—the information in a journal article is more current than that in most books and textbooks (secondary sources).

NEWSPAPERS

Similar to magazines, newspapers may be a good source of ideas to write about and may lead you to the original, primary resources. But unless your scientific writing assignment is about a current event, you will not often be citing newspapers.

REFERENCE BOOKS

Reference books can be a wonderful resource of secondary sources that provide original references and interpretations of others' work. Reference books are often comprehensive and can provide citations to key or seminal works in a particular field. Your introductory psychology textbook may well be one of the most useful reference books you own because it covers a wide range of topics in psychology.

BOOKS

Books, especially primary sources, can be quite valuable in scientific writing. Books give an author the opportunity to expound in greater detail on a particular theory or how variables interact in a complex fashion. Books are not typically as up to date as journal articles because of the increased lead time necessary to publish a book. Also, you will sometimes encounter edited books, in which each chapter is written by a different author. These edited books can be extremely valuable in your search for sources because they often provide multiple and diverse perspectives on some aspect of the same problem or topic.

INTERNET SOURCES

There are a number of search engines available on the Internet that can help a student uncover research related to a paper topic (such as Google or Google Scholar). Internet searches may lead you to original, primary resources or to secondary sources. When retrieving information from the Internet, take care to evaluate its source (which is often difficult to determine). Later in this chapter, I present some standards for you to consider when evaluating research sources from any medium.

KNOWLEDGEABLE FACULTY

Don't forget about your department faculty members! Depending on the course, your instructor may have more expertise in the topic you are writing about than you know. Other faculty members are also likely to know something about your topic or at least be able to point you in the direction of additional primary and secondary sources.

REFERENCE LIBRARIAN

A reference librarian has special talents that can be particularly useful to you as you use the library to obtain the research necessary for your scientific writing assignment. A reference librarian is someone who is educated and trained to help others locate reference materials. At larger schools, there may be a reference librarian specifically for psychology or the social sciences. Don't overlook this valuable resource on your campus.

In addition to the numerous research strategies presented, I have found that students often implement a systematic library research strategy (Landrum & Muench, 1994). In a study of such strategies, I identified four specific approaches that students use for library research: (a) person-specific strategies, in which students build self-confidence and library skills; (b) library-specific strategies, in which students learn what is available to them and how to use their library; (c) paper-specific strategies, in which students learn to understand the details of writing the paper and how library resources can help them; and (d) reference-specific strategies, in which students learn how to use journal articles and books in the library. I point out these library strategies because your research and writing approach may differ, depending on the type of class, type of instructor, or even type of assignment. Adapt to the needs of the assignment. For instance, in a history of psychology class, the emphasis may be more on classic works, focusing on books; however, in a social psychology class, your instructor may want the latest research published in journals. Not only may your strategies be course specific, but they may also be instructor specific. Try to find out what types of source your instructor prefers. In my research methods course, I want students to focus mainly on journal articles because they tend to be the major currency in experimental psychology. Our writing maxim also applies to types of research source.

Evaluating Sources

Once you've completed your library search and gathered (or at least examined) possible research and other sources for your paper, and before careful analysis and extraction of information, you'll need to determine the value or validity of the sources you've gathered. This can be a very important part of any scientific writing assignment, and development of this skill is valuable for any type of future psychology majors pursue. For some types of information, evaluating the veracity of a source is easy. Because of the peer-review process, we have confidence in journal articles that are published in scholarly journals. Books published by reputable, well-known sources allow for confidence in the information they present. For other sources, however—such as information from the Internet—evaluation is crucial. I suggest you consider three evaluative areas when examining sources, suggested in part by Harris (2005) and Kirk (1996).

AUTHORSHIP AND EXPERTISE

Authorship is an essential consideration when using a source for a scientific paper. Sometimes the information may come from a Web site, brochure, or pamphlet, and authorship is difficult to ascertain. This is a problem. If no one is willing to "own" the information, how valuable can it be? To determine the author's expertise, you must know who he or she is. The author may be a corporate entity, which is fine, but authorship should be acknowledged so that you can understand the original source of the information and any particular point of view or bias that the author may have.

CURRENCY AND TIMELINESS

Depending on the type of paper you are writing, currency may be important. If you are writing a literature review of the developments in an area of social psychology in the past 10 years, then timeliness of your sources is obviously an important concern. If you are writing a term paper about some school of thought in psychology's historical development (e.g., structuralism), then the currency of information may not be as important in evaluating sources.

ACCURACY AND CORROBORATION

On the basis of what you have read from other sources, are the findings presently accurate and without bias? Does a new or controversial idea put forth by an author place that idea in the context of previous literature? Is corroboration possible with the ideas presented—for example, have others considered this idea or have replication studies on the topic been completed? Are the sources of the ideas documented by a knowledge of previous work?

When extracting information from the Internet, it is essential to evaluate each source using these standards. Once you are confident that a source is valid, then it's time to critically read the source and extract information you might use in your own scientific writing assignment.

Which Information Is Most Pertinent?

You've done your research and gathered sources that you believe are valid and that you think will be helpful to your paper. It's now time to begin to critically read and analyze your sources so that you can decide what pieces of information may be pertinent to your writing assignment. There is no right or wrong way to do this, and there are numerous approaches. The key is to structure the way you gather information to facilitate its use in your paper. If you organize your ideas beforehand, composition will seem easy. Having a method of note taking allows you to scan through many potential sources systematically; then, when you integrate multiple sources from your research, your paper will show signs of scholarly writing. The difference between a good paper and an excellent paper is often the level of synthesis. Chances are that when you feel that you've exhausted the literature and know your topic inside and out, you will do a good job of synthesizing research for your paper. By using the notecard method (or some variation of it), writers organize their thoughts and ideas beforehand rather than while they are writing.

Here I present an extended example of how to take notes and transition into composing the paper: the notecard method. This method involves noting single ideas on 4-in. × 6-in. index cards and coding those ideas to their sources, which are noted on 3-in. × 5-in. index cards. This method can be adapted to a number of different computer applications and still be tactile (i.e., if you print out your notes and physically shuffle their order), or it can be entirely paperless. A number of computer-oriented alternatives to the notecard method are summarized at the end of this chapter.

STEP 1: SELECT A PAPER TOPIC

Try to generate a topic that interests you, but keep within the confines of the instructor's assignment. The challenge is to select as specific a topic as possible for which there are library materials readily available. Try to decide on a paper topic after examining what your library has to offer. This approach allows you to make sure that there are adequate resources available before you are totally committed to a topic.

STEP 2: CREATE AN OUTLINE

Sketch an outline of the major points you want to make in your paper. Again, this step should be done after taking a quick look at the available library materials. You may already know what kinds of points you want to make, but the library quick search may give you more ideas. Try to be as concrete and specific as possible in your outline. With certain types of scientific writing, your outline may already be prepared for you (Introduction, Method, Results, and Discussion).

STEP 3: MAKE REFERENCE NOTECARDS

On 3-in. × 5-in. index cards, create your reference list or bibliography. Place only one reference on each card, and in the upper right corner give each reference a code (A, B, C, etc.). This code will link each idea card (discussed next) to its source. Write each reference in American Psychological Association (APA) style (more details about APA format for references are provided in chapter 4). The *Publication Manual* (APA, 2010) has very specific reference formats, and book references are formatted differently than journal references; be sure to note the differences. Writing the reference notecard in APA format saves you time later when you type your paper's reference section, and including only one reference per card makes it easy to alphabetize your references. For examples of what a reference notecard might look like, see Figures 3.1, 3.2, and 3.3. Note that the cards presented in the figures have been reduced for print.

FIGURE 3.1

Salant, P. & Dillman, D.A. (1994)

How to conduct your own survey.

New York, NY: Wiley.

Here's a 3-in. × 5-in. reference notecard, approximately to scale. Notice how it is already in APA format, with the hanging indent, double-spacing, and even the attempt to write in italics. This is APA format for referencing a book.

FIGURE 3.2

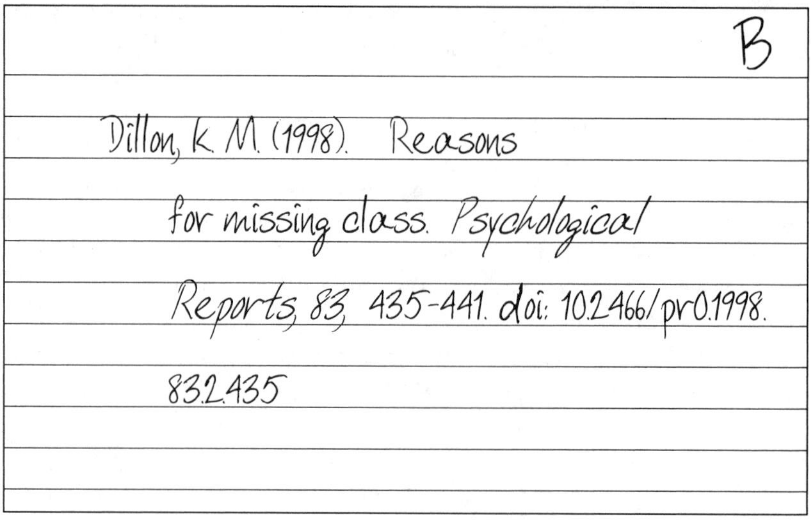

B

Dillon, K. M. (1998). Reasons

for missing class. *Psychological*

Reports, 83, 435-441. doi: 10.2466/pr0.1998.

83.2.435

Here's another reference notecard, reduced in size. This comes from a journal article. It is as close to APA format as can be handwritten, including the journal name and volume number in italics.

FIGURE 3.3

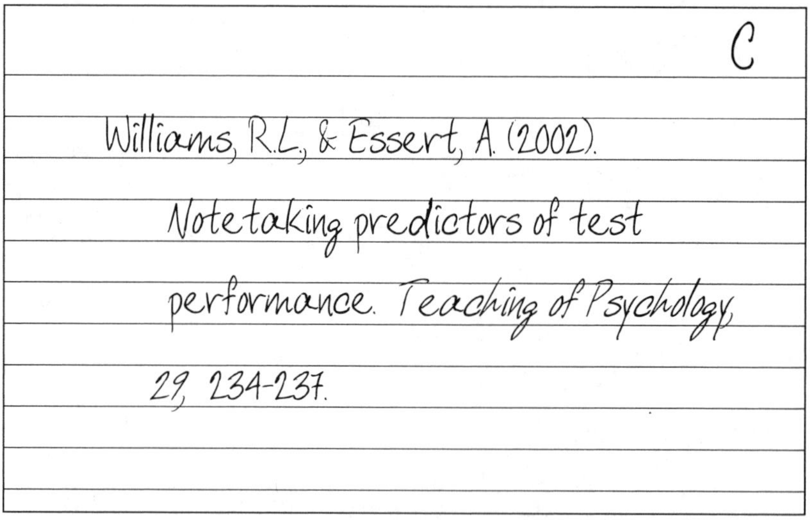

C

Williams, R.L., & Essert, A. (2002).

Notetaking predictors of test

performance. *Teaching of Psychology,*

29, 234-237.

Here's one more example of a reference notecard, with two authors. Note the ampersand (&) rather than the word *and*. Also, this format is specific to a journal article. If this source had been retrieved electronically or by some other method, the details listed on the reference notecard would be different, just as the APA reference would be different.

STEP 4: MAKE IDEA NOTECARDS (NOTES ON SOURCES)

On 4-in. × 6-in. index cards, take your notes on each source or reference you have selected. On each card, write only one idea that you think you might use in your paper (later on, this will facilitate the organization of your paper). For Reference A, you may have four separate ideas you might incorporate into your paper, and you would label them A1, A2, A3, and A4, respectively (see Figures 3.4 and 3.5 for examples of idea notecards). If you think you might like to use the idea in a direct quote, be sure to note the page number on the idea notecard (see Figures 3.6 and 3.7).

STEP 5: PLAN THE PAPER

Before you actually begin writing the paper, plan its course. With your revised outline and your idea notecards, organize your paper by selecting ideas (notecards) and grouping them together. Lay out the course of the paper by physically placing your 4-in. × 6-in. idea notecards in the order in which you are going to use them. How do you know what order? Your outline (Step 2) is your general road map.

FIGURE 3.4

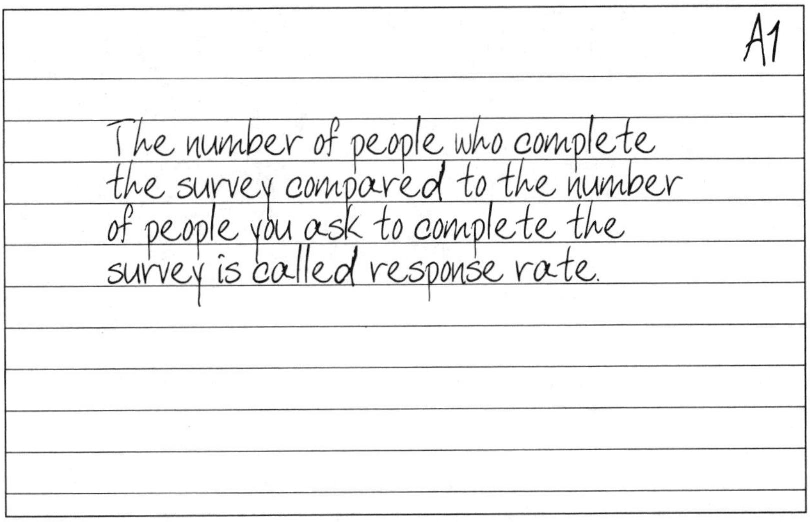

> A1
>
> The number of people who complete the survey compared to the number of people you ask to complete the survey is called response rate.

This is a 4-in. × 6-in. idea notecard, from Reference A. Put only one idea on each idea notecard. This idea is a paraphrase from the book cited.

FIGURE 3.5

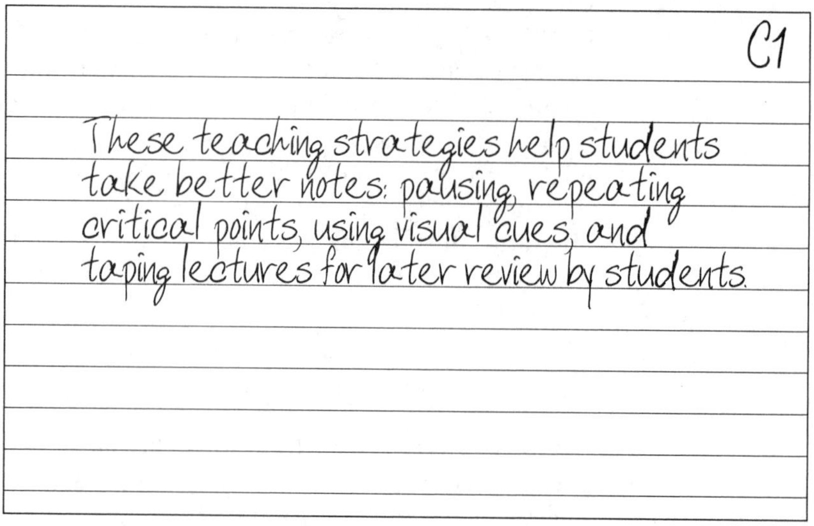

C1

These teaching strategies help students take better notes: pausing, repeating critical points, using visual cues, and taping lectures for later review by students.

Here's an idea notecard from the reference in Figure 3.3 that is a summary of the original idea in the journal article.

FIGURE 3.6

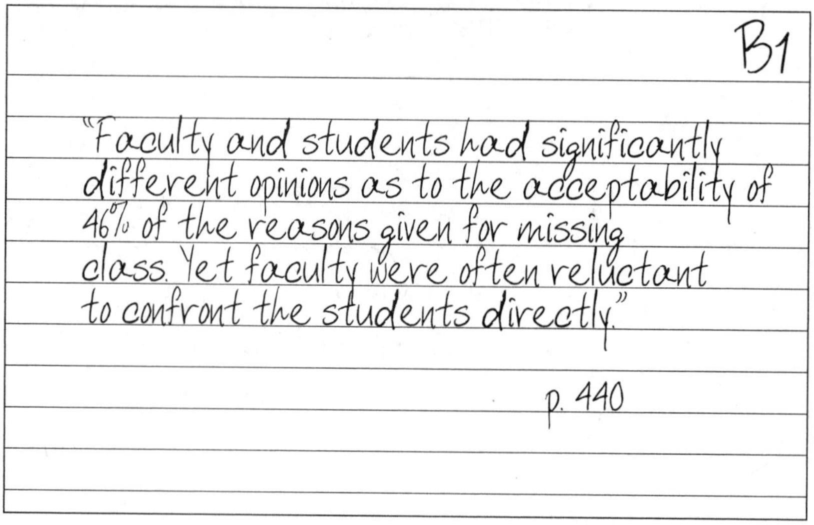

B1

"Faculty and students had significantly different opinions as to the acceptability of 46% of the reasons given for missing class. Yet faculty were often reluctant to confront the students directly."

p. 440

Here's an example of an idea notecard from the reference in Figure 3.2, but this is a direct quote. Note that I placed the exact page number on the idea notecard. When preparing your APA format manuscript, you'll need to cite this page number in the text of your paper.

FIGURE 3.7

C2

"The independent variables include two note taking domains (reading and class lectures) and three dimensions of note taking (completeness, length, and accuracy)."

p. 235

One last example of a idea notecard; again, this is a direct quote with the page number recorded for later use. Also remember that you don't have to use the direct quote; you could turn this idea into a paraphrase, but you must still give credit to the original author.

Try to integrate the paper as much as possible (i.e., don't talk about all the ideas from your A reference, then your B reference, etc.). The whole point of this system is to help you synthesize (integrate) similar ideas from different contexts.

STEP 6: WRITE THE ROUGH DRAFT

Now it's time to actually start writing the paper. Of course, you've already done much of the writing, which has helped you to become very familiar with your reference materials and the points you want to make. In later chapters, we'll revisit this topic as I present specific guidelines and suggestions for writing literature reviews and research papers. Following your paper plan, write the text by following the notecards you've already organized. You need to make the text readable, providing the necessary transition between ideas. A reference list is typically not required with a rough draft (it normally appears at the end of the paper), although you should cite your sources in the text of the paper in APA format. Also, be sure to include a title with your rough draft.

See whether your instructor will review your rough draft without assigning a grade. If this option is not available (and it may not be in larger classes), try to get one of your classmates to read your paper. If you're not sure about something, try it; the worst that can happen in the draft stage is that you receive some free advice. If you see a lot of red ink on your returned draft, think of this, too, as free advice (and on the topic of advice, don't forget about the resources available at your campus writing center). Remember, the rough draft is not the final version; the comments should help to improve your paper. At some point, we all need outside consultants to help us improve and sharpen our skills.

Quite frankly, the notecard method works. By reading, understanding, and analyzing your sources to extract information, taking notes on those sources, and then using those notes in writing your paper, you become better acquainted with the topic. Your understanding of what you are writing about becomes deeper and less superficial. To receive the most benefit from the notecard method, consider the following three strategies for your idea notecards.

Keeping Track of Ideas

Essentially, there are three different strategies to use when you are taking notes on your sources—quoting, paraphrasing, and summarizing (Harris, 2005; University of Maryland University College, 2005b). Harris (2005) offered a number of situations in which you would be interested in using a direct quotation from another source in your own work: expert declaration (a quote from an authority figure), direct support, effective language (the elegance and clarity of the author's words), historical flavor, specific example, controversial statement, or material for analysis. Direct quotes should be used sparingly, and be sure to adhere to the instructor's assignment guidelines. For example, when I teach research methods, students preparing the formal research paper are told they cannot use more than three direct quotes. I do this so that students will realize that scholarly writing does not involve a string of quotations; rather, it involves the interpretation and communication of ideas in the proper form. A string of direct quotations in a paper essentially means that other authors "wrote" your paper.

You should use a direct quotation when an author has said something so eloquently (i.e., effective language) that a paraphrase or a summary would lessen the meaning or impact of the original statement. When you are recording your idea notecards, if you even think you might use a direct quote, write the direct quote on the 4-in. × 6-in. idea notecard, *and note the page number from the original source.* In APA format, the use of a direct quotation also requires that you report the page number (or in some cases, paragraph number) from the quotation source. Also, if you use a long quote (40 words or more), APA format requires that the quote be indented in the text (see pp. 92, 170–174 of the *Publication Manual* for more specific details; APA, 2010). One last concern about quoting is that you should not quote from one source too often (Harris, 2005), especially if the goal of the assignment is for you to integrate and summarize previous research; quoting (or even citing) the same source over and over again shows no review of the literature or synthesis of ideas from multiple sources. Using the notecard method and writing down a single idea on each 4-in. × 6-in. card allows you to easily reorganize ideas into sections and paragraphs, and thus when you are actually ready to do the writing, you have already synthesized your ideas.

A paraphrase is very different from a direct quotation in that a paraphrase is a translation of the writer's original words into your own words, using roughly the same number of words (Harris, 2005; University of Maryland University College, 2005b). Paraphrasing is seen as more scholarly than using direct quotes because it demonstrates a deeper understanding of the original work; in fact, it is quite a talent to be able to take others' ideas and convert them into a less complex or more clear form (it is an important part of what good teachers do). Paraphrasing allows you to reword, simplify, or clarify the original writer's meaning. When using the notecard method, most of your idea notecards should be paraphrased.

A summary is similar to a paraphrase in that you translate the author's original words into your own; however, a summary is shorter than the original (Harris, 2005). Key benefits to summaries include simplifying and condensing the author's original ideas. Summaries are also a good strategy when you are extracting information for your idea notecards.

Whether you are using a direct quote, paraphrase, or summary, the key benefit in connecting your idea notecards to your reference notecards is to give credit where credit is due. This is essential in scientific writing, and failure to do so means plagiarism, which can have serious repercussions (more on plagiarism later).

Keeping Track of Sources

The references that you gather using your 3-in. × 5-in. reference notecards are more important than you might originally think. A reference list shows off your "academic pedigree," that is, it shows the line of thinking and research that you followed to place your current work in its proper context. Often, your instructor will know how much effort you have put into your writing assignment by examining the extent of the references you have cited in your paper. The reference list should be meticulously prepared (and note that there are many different APA format rules for the different types of materials you might reference). Later chapters in this book thoroughly review the proper preparation of reference citations in APA format.

In other courses with a writing component, you may be asked to prepare papers or reports using Modern Language Association (MLA) format. MLA format is commonly taught in high schools and in college-level English classes. Unfortunately, MLA format differs vastly from APA format, although some of the underlying goals of scholarly writing are the same. One important way in which MLA and APA differ significantly is in the use of references. In APA format, when you cite a reference in the text, you use the author's last name (or, if there are several authors, names) followed by the year of publication. In MLA format, the author's name is usually followed by the number of the page in the original source from which the information was taken. In APA format, you have a References page, which lists every reference cited in the main text of the paper. At the end of an MLA paper, you might have a Works Cited page, and see frequent notations like *ibid.* and *op. cit.* If you were preparing a Bibliography (or Works Consulted page), it would list every reference article you consulted, whether or not it was cited in the text of the paper. As always, be sure to heed your instructor's advice and be sure to use the referencing method that he or she prefers.

MAXIMIZING THE NOTECARD METHOD

It may appear that the notecard method involves much work, and it does. But the benefits are clear in that you will better understand the research materials *before* you start writing your paper. You will have read the materials, evaluated the sources, and then used direct quotes from, paraphrased, or summarized the primary source material. Then you will start the actual writing of the first draft of your writing assignment. The notecard method works best if you follow it completely; that is, for every reference you examine, you create a reference notecard, and for every idea you think you might want to use, you create an idea notecard. If you take the time to do this up front, it greatly facilitates creating the final product. You don't want to be scrambling for the journal title or volume at the last minute when you are typing up your references, and if you filled out a reference notecard, you won't need to. You won't lose points for not providing the page number for a direct quote if you fully completed your idea notecard because the page number will be on it. Rearranging the reference notecards into alphabetical order will make typing your Reference section easy—you can do it straight from the notecards. Recording a single idea on an idea notecard will make it an easy task to organize, arrange, and rearrange ideas into a coherent story, complete with reference material and integrated in such a way as to demonstrate your scholarly writing ability. To this day, I still use my own variation of the notecard method because it leads to better synthesis of ideas and enhanced clarity.

Alternate Methods of Recording and Using Research Notes

To be honest, my own variation of the notecard method involves using Microsoft Word, and I no longer physically write all of this information on actual index cards (part of the reason is efficiency—my handwriting is awful!) There are a number of variations possible, but the essential ideas remain—carefully track your resource materials and deal with ideas one at a time. In this last section, I present some technology-based alternatives to using actual 3-in. × 5-in. and 4-in. × 6-in. index cards.

Even though I like the old-school notecard method (actual paper index cards), there are disadvantages to it. There are now a number of computer-based alternatives available for use. Some of these techniques make use of existing computer programs, and others are programs specifically designed for note taking and writing. The advantages to taking your notes via a computer program include the ability to (a) download from Web sites directly into a note file, (b) cut and paste data directly, (c) move information around electronically rather than physically, (d) have a legible set of notes no matter what your hand-writing is like, and (e) cut and paste bibliographic information directly (Wiley Publishing, 2007). However, in continuing with our fairness theme, there are also disadvantages to computer note taking: (a) You actually have to take your notes at a computer; (b) you must back up your notes after every session or else risk losing your work; (c) you must scroll to see your work, making seeing the big picture a difficult task; (d) you must spend time moving bits of information around using cut and paste until your ideas are in the order you want, and (e) you must interrupt your reading to go enter notes on a computer (Wiley Publishing, 2007). Some of these disadvantages also apply to the paper version, such as interrupting your reading to take notes on index cards. In the end, you'll need to experiment with different approaches to see what works best for you.

You can use existing software programs to customize your own computer-based note-taking approach. I use Microsoft Word to organize my references and my ideas and to integrate them into something I am writing. However, I am one of those people who likes the tactile ability to move things around. Thus, after typing them into Word, I usually print out the idea notes and move them around physically until they are in an order I like, although I could do the same thing on a computer screen. You might also use Microsoft Excel or Microsoft Access. Forrest (n.d.) suggests using Microsoft PowerPoint. The nice feature of this approach is that once the notecards are created as separate slides, you can easily use the slide sorter feature in PowerPoint to arrange your ideas (slides) in any order you wish. By including the bibliographic information in the header of each slide, the reference and idea notecards are combined. This appears to be a very nice alternative to using actual paper notecards if you are so electronically inclined.

There are other, specialized note-taking programs as well. Microsoft offers a specialized program, OneNote (Microsoft Corporation, 2007), to assist in note taking and information management. Some of the features of OneNote include the ability to capture Web pages, hyperlinking, using file attachments, creating tables, and access to drawing tools; it can also recognize text embedded in pictures (Microsoft Corporation, 2007). Using this program has the added benefit of direct integration with other Microsoft programs you may be using. Another software alternative is Nota Bene (Nota Bene, n.d.), which is designed for academic research and writing, with numerous tools to handle word processing, organize a general database and a bibliographic database (all of your references), a search engine, and more. A less complex alternative to OneNote and Nota Bene is ndxCards (TruTamil, 2004), which allows you to electronically take notes and then export those notes (and reference list information) to a word processor.

Be sure to select an approach that meets your basic needs without being too complicated. Whichever approach you use, the bottom line is to be able to consider ideas individually and to sort those ideas while preserving the source from which the idea came. The notecard method spans beyond academic writing into other genres of writing, including scriptwriting (remember, telling a good story is our common thread, even for scientific writing). Mindola Software (2006) offers a software program called supernotecard for scriptwriting that allows the writer to create outlines, define characters, and be able to manipulate information in a nonlinear fashion. Using some variation of the notecard method in your own scientific writing will help you tell a better story!

How to Write Your Psychology Paper With Style: General Tips

4

Well, then, I propose to you that, English Literature being (as we agreed) an Art, with a living and therefore improvable language for its medium or vehicle, a part— and no small part—of our business is *to practise it.* Yes, I seriously propose to you that here in Cambridge we *practise writing:* that we practise it not only for our own improvement, but to make, or at least try to make, appropriate, perspicuous, accurate, persuasive writing a recognisable hall-mark of anything turned out by our English School.

—*Sir Arthur Quiller-Couch,* On the Art of Writing

Now that you've gathered all your research notes and determined more or less how they will fit into your outline, I want to zoom out again and reexamine the guiding principles behind the writing endeavor you've embarked on. These guiding principles are what underpin scientific writing style, which we examine in this chapter. Why are you writing, aside from the fact that your instructor assigned you something to write? Ultimately, as a psychology student, you are writing to get a taste of what professional psychologists do, even if you never become a professional psychologist yourself. As stated in chapter 1, professional psychologists continue threads of scientific discovery; however, to do this they have to communicate what they have discovered. They have to determine whether a particular paper will represent a true contribution to knowledge. Your instructors may not expect you to become a professional psychologist, but they do attempt to model the intellectual demands and critical thinking skills necessary to be a psychologist. So, how do you know whether your paper will contribute to the scientific knowledge base? Sternberg (2005) has outlined eight ways to determine this:

1. The paper contains one or more surprising results that nevertheless make sense in some theoretical context. Whatever outcome occurs, you need to try to make sense of it, especially in the context of your study. For example, my research methods students often attempt to replicate a common finding and fail to do so. The most common reason for this is that their study did not have enough participants. Thus, they are able to make sense of an outcome they were not expecting.

2. The results presented in the paper are of major theoretical or practical significance. The best way for you to achieve this is to study an important topic. If you are studying an important topic, then the results have a good chance of being important as well.

3. The ideas in the paper are new and exciting, perhaps presenting a new way of looking at an old problem. Students are often very good at achieving this because they can bring a fresh perspective to a problem or issue that psychologists tend to look at the same old way. Taking a unique approach to studying a problem is where your scientific creativity kicks in.

4. The interpretation of results is unambiguous. This is where you get to apply the information you have learned from your course or courses in statistics. Using the appropriate descriptive and inferential statistics, you can draw conclusions about the problem being studied and have some certainty in your conclusion. Developing scientific, testable hypotheses allows the use of both quantitative and qualitative methods to interpret conclusions with clarity.

5. The paper integrates into a new, simpler framework data that had previously required a complex, possibly unwieldy framework. The ability to simplify complex relationships, when possible, is highly desirable in science, and this notion is sometimes referred to as *Occam's razor*. Occam's razor suggests that when two theories make the same prediction, the simpler theory is preferred to the more complex theory (Hiroshi, 1997). If your research can make this contribution, you have provided a highly valuable service to science.

6. The paper contains a major debunking of previously held ideas. To accomplish this goal, a good approach for students is to select a myth or urban legend to test in their research study. Scientists

are drawn to counterintuitive findings (the opposite of what is expected), so if you can debunk a myth or negate an urban legend, others will find value in your work.

7. The paper presents an experiment with a particularly clever paradigm or experimental manipulation. If you can develop a new or innovative method of studying a complex phenomenon, the approach or methodology you use can almost be as valuable as the findings. Because psychology shares its trade secrets in the Method sections of journal articles, your contribution becomes public once you publish a journal article. Innovative ways of thinking about human behavior can lead to innovative approaches to studying that behavior in the laboratory or in the field.

8. The findings or theory presented in the paper are general ones. You can achieve this in your writing by not overreaching with your conclusions. From the storytelling perspective, this happens in Act 3, where the climax occurs and the plot twist is resolved. Your research paper should end with broad statements that provide a general conclusion to what you have discovered through the course of your project.

Good scientists are good communicators. For their contribution to the scientific knowledge base to be accepted by other scientists, they must also use good storytelling technique. That is, they make conscious choices about such things as how they will describe the main players in the story, the tone and approach to the story itself, and the order in which they will narrate events. As mentioned in chapter 1, the writer is not central to the scientific story; the topic is the main character, and in psychology the topic is usually behavior. Objectivity is the hallmark of scientific writing, so the tone reflects distance from the topic, and the linear order of presentation reflects a thinking process that values measurable hypotheses and results above opinion. Of course, psychologists do include opinions in their writing, but this is usually done when presenting the hypothesis, which is then dispassionately accepted or rejected.

Style, both in a general sense and an American Psychological Association (APA) sense, actually simplifies some of the decision making that goes into scientific writing. Although the specifics of any particular writing assignment may differ, you will find that there are commonalities among types of scientific writing assignments in psychology. This chapter explores those common factors and how they may apply to particular writing assignments. Applying these general tips to idiosyncratic assignments is how you practice good writing, to borrow a phrase from the quotation that opens this chapter.

Why Instructors Like
to Read Stylish Papers

Instructors of undergraduate and graduate psychology majors teach APA style because that is our gold standard. Baker and Henrichsen (2002, para. 3) said it better:

> In academic writing, the reader's response to a piece of writing is crucial. In a classroom situation the reader is also usually the teacher, and at least part of a paper's grade is generally based on how well it follows the accepted style. Proper formatting is the hallmark of a detail-oriented researcher. A writer who makes stylesheet errors because he or she believes they are "no big deal" might be surprised when evaluators question other details of the paper, such as the data on which the conclusions are based. After all—if a writer can't get all the periods in the right places, how can he or she be expected to correctly calculate an ANOVA or t-test?

The *Publication Manual* (APA, 2010) actually serves two functions: It is a style manual—that is, it addresses sentence structure issues, grammar, how to compose paragraphs, and so forth—and it is also a presentation guide—that is, it addresses how the manuscript should appear on paper (Scribe, 2012). For the sake of clarity, I refer to *APA style* as the mode of expression and *APA format* as the mode of presentation. Both topics are covered in detail in this book: APA formatting issues are addressed in this chapter; in chapters 5 and 6 concerning literature reviews and research papers, respectively, issues of both APA style and APA formatting are further explored.

Just how important is it to prepare a manuscript using APA style and format? Obviously, the answer will vary, depending on the instructor and the instructor's assignment. Remember, though, that the *Publication Manual* was originally created for psychologists wanting to publish their work in scholarly journals. The editor of a journal is the person ultimately responsible for deciding what gets published and what does not. Do journal editors really care about APA style and format, or is it just a formality? Brewer, Scherzer, Van Raalte, Petitpas, and Andersen (2001) asked just that question of hundreds of psychology journal editors, and the result are interesting. As it turns out, to some journal editors APA format is extremely important: "39% of the respondents reported that they *had* returned a manuscript to an author purely for failing to adhere to APA style" (p. 266). When asked about the most common problems, the journal editors listed the top three problem areas as references, tables and figures, and mathematics and statistics. This subset of editors who desired strict adherence to APA style were labeled "APA style sticklers" (Brewer et al., 2001, p. 267).

Many types of scientific writing in psychology share components of the same overall style. In later chapters, I address very specific details about assignments and their particular requirements, but it is useful to review here the general style that is used for most scientific writing. Exhibit 4.1 provides a quick overview of the general sections you may be asked to write.

The ability to write clearly and concisely is an essential skill in becoming a good scientist. Throughout this book, I emphasize the importance of clarity and the ability to tell a coherent story. Psychologists do follow the *Publication Manual* as a general guide, and the *Publication Manual* provides detailed information about the style that scientific writing should follow and the format in which it should appear. However, the 272-page *Publication Manual* still offers this advice to students: Many psychology departments require that student papers, theses, and dissertations be prepared according to the *Publication Manual.* Of course, where departmental

---

EXHIBIT 4.1

Typical Sections of an American Psychological Association–Style Research Paper

Title page (take credit)
   Author's name and affiliation.
   Other information as your professor requests.
   Page numbering (header) and running head.
Abstract (quick summary)
   Typically range from 150–250 words.
   Some assignments will not require an abstract.
Introduction (what you are studying)
   Introduce the research problem (or thesis statement).
   Develop the background.
   State the purpose and rationale for the paper.
Method (what you did)
   Participants, materials, and procedure.
   Should be in enough detail to replicate work if desired.
Results (what happened)
   Presentation of statistical outcomes; tables and figures if necessary.
   Presentation, not interpretation.
Discussion (what it means)
   Was there support for the research idea?
   Did the study help resolve the original problem?
   What conclusions can be drawn?
   Suggest improvements and avenues for further or new research.
Reference section (give credit where credit is due)
   Authors listed alphabetically by last name; no first names used, only initials.
   Be sure all citations in the text are referenced.
   Shows your scholarly ability and how you did your background research.

requirements differ from those in the *Publication Manual,* the departmental or institutional requirements take precedence. At its essence, the *Publication Manual* is the instruction guide to authors on how to communicate psychological findings to the scientific community.

In this chapter, I highlight some of the most common areas of concern for writing in APA style and format. Obviously, the *Publication Manual* is the comprehensive source that addresses almost every possible nuance of a research-paper-writing situation you may face. I was selective in what I chose to address here; these are the big issues that will get you going, and you can refer to your *Publication Manual* for the details I did not address here. For instance, the rules for preparing a figure in APA format are very precise (in fact, part of an entire book is devoted to preparing figures; Nicol & Pexman, 2010); however, figures are often not necessary for undergraduate writing projects.

MANUSCRIPT PREPARATION

One of the most important things for you to remember when handing in a paper for any college class is that it is a representation of the quality of your skills and abilities. Every time you hand in an assignment, make sure it is your very best work. If you are handing in a rough draft of a section of your research paper, and the ink smudges on any of the pages, reprint that page. If the dog started eating your homework, redo or recopy that page. When you hand in work that appears sloppy, some professors may jump to the conclusion that your work is also sloppy. You would never dream of sending a resume to a prospective employer that had typographical errors or coffee stains on it—why would you do so for your instructors? Be sure to follow these rules for manuscript preparation in APA format, but also be sure to heed any exceptions that the instructor gives you.

WORD PROCESSING: TYPING AND LAYOUT

With regard to how the page looks when complete, here are the main ideas for the layout of the page in APA format:

- Use a 12-point Times New Roman font.
- Double-space everything, but you can use single- or double-spacing in tables and figures.
- Set 1-in. margins at the top, bottom, left, and right of the page.
- Certain parts of a research paper start on a new page: title page, abstract, introduction, references, appendixes, tables, figure captions, and figures.
- Every page is numbered. Use the automatic functions of your word-processing program to generate running heads and page

numbers for your file. In the example paper in Figure 7.4, you will see how this looks.

- In front of the page number, you will include the first two to three words of the manuscript title, followed by five spaces. This feature is also presented in the sample paper.
- Indent each paragraph ½ in. (this is usually the default setting).
- In proper APA format, use one space after commas, colons, semicolons, periods in the reference section, and periods in the initials of a person's name. Use one or two spaces after end-of-sentence punctuation. This is one of those rules that some instructors may allow you to break (personally, I like two spaces after the end of a sentence because I think it improves readability).

HEADINGS AND SERIES

Headings are used to help organize the flow of the text and to give readers signposts for where they are in the midst of the manuscript. In the sample paper at the end of chapter 7, you will see the typical three levels of heading used in APA papers. (The *Publication Manual* actually presents variations from one to five levels of heading.) The headings are differentiated by capital or lowercase letters, boldface, italics, centered text, and so forth.

Seriation refers to the presentation of multiple items within a sentence, for example, whether you are providing a step-by-step sequence (1-2-3) or just listing different items (a-b-c). The rules for seriation are straightforward: When the individual items within a series do not contain a comma, use commas to separate them (e.g., "The key items to remember are (a) be honest, (b) be brave, and (c) be true"). If the individual items within a series do contain a comma, use semicolons to separate them (e.g., "To pilot test the new instrument, we (a) generated a list of potential items, based on participant interviews; (b) developed potential survey items, using a Likert-type scale; and (c) completed the survey with volunteers from a college course in psychometrics").

ABBREVIATIONS AND NUMBERS

Like many scientists, psychologists tend to use jargon specific to the discipline. Often, jargon is expressed in the form of abbreviations. The *Publication Manual* advises using abbreviations sparingly. There are places where repeating a particular phrase (e.g., *cumulative final exam score*) is cumbersome and using an abbreviation makes sense (e.g., *CFES*). Be careful in assuming that an abbreviation is so common that all readers will know what it means. In general, spell out an abbreviation the first time it is used, with the abbreviation in parentheses afterward. Then you can use the abbreviation (without parentheses) throughout the remainder of your paper. Be sure to use the appropriate scientific abbreviations in text; the *Publication Manual* lists these on pages 108–110 (APA, 2010). If you choose to use Latin abbreviations, remember that they are not italicized. Table 4.1 contains these helpful abbreviations, their meanings, and how they are used (APA, 2010, p. 108; Plonsky, 2006). These abbreviations are only used within parentheses, with the exception of *et al.*, which is used inside or outside parentheses.

To be honest, the use of numbers in an APA-formatted paper is confusing. There are general rules, but there appear to be as many exceptions as there are rules. Generally speaking, numbers below 10 are typically spelled out as words (zero, one, two, three, four, etc.) and numbers above 10 are usually expressed as numerals (10, 11, 12, 13, etc.). The under-10 rule also does not apply in the use of numbers in the abstract of your research paper (numerals are used for all numbers in the abstract) or in numbers that represent time, dates, ages, scores and points on a scale, exact sums of money, and numerals as numerals. Also remember that if you start a sentence with a number, you must spell out the number in words and use proper capitalization (e.g., "Thirty-two general psychology students completed the survey"). In

TABLE 4.1

Latin Abbreviations

Abbreviation	What it means	Sample sentence
cf.	compare	APA format and style based on the *Publication Manual* are designed to provide scientific notation to researcher's ideas (cf. expression of ideas with the *Chicago Manual of Style*).
e.g.	for example	There are different types of doctoral degrees in psychology (e.g., PhD, PsyD, and EdD).
etc.	and so forth	There are numerous variables that influence a student's decision to attend college (such as school prestige, amount of financial aid, distance from home, availability of a major, etc.).
i.e.	that is	There is not much evidence that seat time (i.e., time on task) is directly related to student performance in the classroom.
viz.	namely	Although there are multiple organizations for psychologists to become involved in, as is the case in other sciences, often the largest organization possesses the greatest degree of political clout (viz., the American Psychological Association).
vs.	versus	Developmental psychologists will probably never completely understand the contributions of heredity and environment (i.e., the nature vs. nurture debate).
et al.	and others	These three authors (Smith et al., 2006) concluded that the impact on low birthweight was greater for children of low-income families as compared with children of high-income families.

general, do your best to avoid starting a sentence with a number. APA format dictates that numerical measurement be expressed in metric units, that is, centimeters and meters rather than inches and feet. For the more explicit rules concerning the use of numbers, see pages 111–114 of the *Publication Manual* (APA, 2010).

CITATIONS AND QUOTATIONS IN TEXT

Good scientific writing places an idea about a variable or behavior in context. That is, part of the story is the backstory that contributes to our current state of knowledge about a phenomenon and, in a research paper, the gap or hole in the knowledge that the research paper strives to fill. To accomplish this goal, however, you must be familiar with the existing literature, which is why you conduct library research on your topic, extract materials using the notecard method, and synthesize those materials, looking for common themes or threads, by arranging your idea notecards into coherent paragraphs. An essential component of this task is the ability to cite the work of others in your own work—in other words, giving credit where credit is due (the inability to give credit would be an instance of plagiarism).

As a psychology student, you are already becoming accustomed to this practice in science. Remember reading your introductory psychology textbook? You would be reading a particular paragraph, and the flowing text would be rudely interrupted by last names and a year, sometimes in parentheses, sometimes not in parentheses. This practice, called *citation* or *citing*, is vital to scientific writing. We must give credit where credit is due. We cannot borrow others' ideas without proper attribution. The ability to cite (and properly cite using APA format) is one way in which you show that you are developing into a scholar. Students sometimes worry that an introduction or a literature review is not very original because it is filled with the citations of others' work. However, the originality comes from how you put those ideas together; your unique contribution is the thread or synthesis or common theme you identified and then documented with your citations! The ability to identify common themes where they exist is a highly sought-after intellectual skill; therefore, using proper citation methods (and reference lists) helps you demonstrate your developing abilities as a scientist.

Although you can imagine that there are many variations on a theme, in APA format there are basically three ways to present citations in the text of your paper: author name(s) and publication year outside of parentheses; author name(s) outside of parentheses, publication year in parentheses; and author name(s) and publication year inside parentheses. How do you decide which format to use? I suggest that you consider the overall flow of the paragraph and make a selection that avoids the passive voice. See Table 4.2 for sample sentences

| TABLE 4.2 | | | |

Examples of Citation Styles With Varying Numbers of Authors

No. of authors or citations	Author and publication year outside of parentheses	Author outside parentheses, publication year inside parentheses	Both author and publication year inside parentheses
One citation, one author only	In 2004, Bem published a comprehensive article addressing critical issues in writing the empirical journal article.	In a recent book, Bem (2004) offered key suggestions for writing the empirical journal article.	Well-organized and pertinent advice about writing the empirical journal article already exists (Bem, 2004).
One citation, more than one author	In 2006, Calderon and Austin offered cogent suggestions for writing in APA style.	An excellent chapter by Calderon and Austin (2006) presents cogent examples of proper use of APA format.	The ability to write clearly in APA style is a marketable skill for students (Calderon & Austin, 2006).

using the variety of forms. There may be occasions when you may need to reference two or more articles in the same sentence. This is usually accomplished inside parentheses. You separate the references with semicolons, and the order of presentation is by first author's last name, not year of publication. An example would look like this: "Excellent advice for preparing research papers in APA format exists in a number of resources (Bem, 2004; Calderon & Austin, 2006)." Note that outside of parentheses, you use *and* between authors' names (or, with three or more authors, just before the last author's name); however, inside parentheses, you use the ampersand (&) between authors' names (or, with three or more authors, just before the last author's name).

As you can imagine, there are also detailed rules for the presentations of quotations in text. You normally use the citation styles above; however, in addition you must report the number of the page on which (or paragraph in which) the quotation appeared (this is why, using the notecard method, you write down on your idea notecard the page number of a passage that you think you might use as a direct quote). Overall, be sure to follow the instructor's preferences for the use of direct quotes in your research paper assignment. As I've alluded to earlier, I am not a fan of direct quotes in research papers—they should be used only when the original author has said something so perfectly that paraphrasing it would not communicate the same thought. I think students sometimes see direct quotes as a way to have to write less, and I often tell my students that a string of direct quotes does not make a scholarly paper. You exhibit your research talent much more clearly when you take a complicated passage and paraphrase it into simpler terms—that is a valuable skill (and, by the way, that's what good teachers do!). If you are going to use direct quotes, be sure to follow the rules of APA format.

For instance, if you plan to use a quote of 40 words or more, you must use a block format in your text to set off the quote (see pp. 91–92, 170–173 of the *Publication Manual;* APA, 2010). If you omit part of a quote, you must note that by using ellipsis marks (. . .) within the quote; however, be sure that your deletion does not change the meaning of the original idea. Remember that you cannot use ellipsis at the beginning or end of a direct quote. If you want to add emphasis to the original quote (e.g., by italicizing a word), you must acknowledge that you added the italics to the text (i.e., that what you have italicized was not in italics in the original quote). If you are quoting from a source with page numbers, then you must report a page number (e.g., "p. 278"). If you are reporting from a source without page numbers (e.g., a brochure or a Web site), you must cite the paragraph number using the paragraph symbol (e.g., para. 7).

TABLES AND FIGURES

There is extensive coverage of table and figure presentation in the *Publication Manual* (APA, 2010). Tables are fairly common in research papers because they can present a large volume of information in an efficient amount of space. Even though tables are efficient, don't over-rely on them; you only want to use a table if it is integral to the story—that is, don't use a table just to say you used a table. Tables need to be explicitly mentioned in your text; often that's in the Method or Results section (e.g., "See Table 1 for the means and standard deviations for the survey items"). Tables are double spaced, just as the rest of your APA-formatted paper is, and cannot contain vertical lines. Table titles are italicized. For more details on table preparation, see *Publication Manual* pages 128–150 (an additional resource is Nicol & Pexman, 2010). I also present more examples of table preparation in chapter 7.

Figures are used in a research paper to present graphical or pictorial information. In the appropriate context, figures can be invaluable aids in telling a complex story, but figure preparation is also complex. Not only are there precise rules for figure preparation, but in APA format a figure also requires a figure caption to explain the figure. The sample sections and complete sample paper in chapter 7 present a typical table, but not a figure. For more explicit details on figure preparation, see pages 151–167 in the *Publication Manual* (APA, 2010) or additional resources such as Nicol and Pexman (2010).

Audience Approval Meter: Ask What You Are Being Graded On

Essentially, the advice I have given you about "giving the instructor the assignment the way he or she wants it" also applies to me when I submit manuscripts for publication in journals. We all have to follow the professional expectations of the discipline when making our work public. At times, this is frustrating because different faculty members (and different journals) may use slightly different criteria in deciding whether a research paper is good or if a manuscript is publishable. The strategy to follow is to find out as much as possible about the evaluation standards of whomever will be reviewing your work. Ideally, with your scientific writing assignments, an instructor may be able to provide a grading rubric before you submit your written work. This rubric will give you an idea of what your instructor's expectations are and what the point values are for particular parts of an assignment. Figures 4.1 and 4.2 contain sample rubrics I use when grading research papers in my research methods course. Figure 4.1 is a rubric for the introduction section of the paper, and Figure 4.2 is a rubric for the final draft.

Telling and Retelling Your Story: Drafting, Editing, Revising, and Proofreading

You'll recall that when journal editors were asked about problem areas of manuscripts submitted for publication by faculty members, the foremost problem area was the references. In later chapters, I present more examples of references, but here is a quick overview of the typical types of reference citations you might have in your reference list. Note that these examples are not comprehensive, and the *Publication Manual* lists 77 different examples! Some of these examples are from Landrum and Davis (2007), and others are from APA at http://www.apastyle.org. Note that these examples are not in absolutely perfect APA format (e.g., there would be 1-in. margins on all four sides of the page, true double-spacing, etc.).

The *Publication Manual* is very specific in its rules, but the overriding principle for a reference citation is that you provide the reader with enough bibliographic information to find the reference, that is, a guide to where you extracted the information. A complete reference citation is important because it allows any reader to retrace the "intellectual journey" that brought you to your conclusions.

FIGURE 4.1

Introduction/Literature Review Check Sheet
PSYC 321 Research Methods

The text of the paper begins with the introduction. The primary function of the introduction is to justify the study described in the report. To help the reader understand why the particular study was conducted, the introduction usually contains the following subsections. Possible points = 75

Grading Areas	Grading Criteria	Grade Points and Designations	Actual Grade
Completion of Assignment (50 points)	**1. An introduction to the topic under study.** Convince the reader that this is an important issue. **2. A brief review of the research findings and theories related to the topic.** Put this research topic in the context of what has been done previously. Show off your scholarly literature search. If nothing is available on your exact topic, be broad. **3. A statement of the problem to be addressed by the research (identifying an area in which knowledge is incomplete).** While reviewing the literature, find a problem or gap in our current knowledge. **4. A statement of the purpose of the present research (to solve the problem identified, but perhaps only a specific part of it).** Tell the reader what part of the problem you are going to solve. **5. A brief description of the method, intended to establish the relationship between the question being addressed and the method used to address it.** In one paragraph, give a brief review of the intended method of the study. **6. A description of any predictions about the outcome and of the hypotheses used to generate those predictions.** Write in complete sentences your working hypotheses, not null hypotheses.	Distinguished (A) = 46-50 Superior (B) = 42-45 Average (C) = 38-41 Below Average (D) = 34-37 Failure (F) = 0-33	
APA Style and Clarity of Presentation (25 points)	■ One-inch margins on all four sides of the page; running head and page number inside the top margin. No right justification of text, 12 pt. serif font throughout, no changes in font or font size. ■ References cited correctly in text either as paraphrases or direct quotes with page numbers; direct quotes used sparingly; lists used sparingly but when used, used in APA format. Credit is given where credit is due (or else it is plagiarism). ■ Spelling, grammar, punctuation, noun-verb agreement all correctly followed; obvious mistakes avoided (paper was proofread). Avoid being colloquial (too informal); no contractions, no abbreviations unless APA-approved. ■ Transitions between sections should be smooth; avoid awkward sentence constructions, write in complete sentences. Text looks good on the paper; black ink on bright white paper, no printer problems. APA *Publication Manual* (6th edition) followed. Stapled in upper left corner.	Distinguished (A) = 23-25 Superior (B) = 21-22 Average (C) = 19-20 Below Average (D) = 17-18 Failure (F) = 0-16	
	TOTAL		

Sample rubric for grading an introduction section.

WRITING THE ROUGH DRAFT

If you have been following the advice of previous chapters, writing your first rough draft will not be so daunting. You have a research question or thesis statement, you have done a review of the literature and gathered your research articles, you have read them carefully while recording your reference notecards and idea notecards, and now you are ready to

FIGURE 4.2

Manuscript Final Draft Check Sheet
PSYC 321 Research Methods

This is the complete, final draft of your manuscript. It is the culmination of an entire semester's worth of work. It should represent your best effort--be proud of your work. Possible points = 150

Grading Areas	Grading Criteria	Grade Points, Designations	Actual Grade
Completion of Assignment (75 points)	• **All the sections of the manuscript are present:** Title page, Abstract, Introduction, Method, Results, Discussion, References, Tables • **All of the instructions from all of the grading sheets, class instructions, course syllabus, and manuscript template have been followed. Previous errors have been corrected in the final draft. Assembled in correct order.**	Distinguished (A) = 69-75 Superior (B) = 63-68 Average (C) = 57-62 Below Average (D) = 51-56 Failure (F) = 0-50	
APA Style and Clarity of Presentation (75 points)	• One inch margins on all four sides of the page; page number inside the top margin. No right justification of text, 12 pt. serif font throughout, no changes in font or font size, double-spaced throughout. Looks perfect, is perfect. • References cited correctly in text either as paraphrases or direct quotes with page numbers; direct quotes used sparingly; lists used sparingly but when used, used in APA format. Credit is given where credit is due (or else it is plagiarism). References in perfect APA format. Every citation is in the references, and spellings match throughout manuscript. 6th edition format followed throughout. • Spelling, grammar, punctuation, noun-verb agreement all correctly followed; obvious mistakes avoided (paper was proofread). Avoid being colloquial (too informal); no contractions, no abbreviations unless APA-approved. Efforts made to make paper readable. Good flow and transitions. • Transitions between sections should be smooth; avoid awkward sentence constructions, write in complete sentences. Text looks good on the paper; black ink on bright white paper, no printer problems. Stapled in upper left corner. **Two copies handed in.**	Distinguished (A) = 69-75 Superior (B) = 63-68 Average (C) = 57-62 Below Average (D) = 51-56 Failure (F) = 0-50	
TOTAL			

Sample rubric for grading a complete APA-formatted manuscript.

write. Because you have placed one idea on each card, you can easily arrange and rearrange your ideas into paragraphs. But at some point, even with all the wonderful background work you have done, it's time to start writing.

As with any important project, sometimes it's hard to get started. Writers (not just student writers) often want the words to come out perfectly the first time around. Although that might be nice, it rarely happens. The overall goal of a rough draft is to get you started, and then later in the process you can edit, revise, and proofread. Being too perfectionistic in your expectations of your first draft may cause you to procrastinate. A little procrastination is okay, but too much will lead to panic and cramming at the last minute, and may not allow you to do your best work. Some helpful suggestions for writing your rough draft follow.

To help avoid procrastination, allow yourself to write an imperfect rough draft. The point is to just get started writing. I often tell my students that it is much easier to edit than to create. However, before you can edit, you first have to generate some content. Staring at a blank page or a blank computer screen can be intimidating—the best cure is to start writing. "Consider a lousy rough draft a good start" (SparkNotes, 2006, para. 4).

You know yourself better than anyone. It may be unreasonable for you to block out time on Saturday from 1:00 p.m. to 7:00 p.m. to "write a rough draft." You know your best times of day; try to do some of your writing during those points in the day. Waiting until 1:00 a.m., when you finally have some time, is also not a good idea. Write in short spurts—promise yourself that you will write nonstop for 15 or 30 minutes, without distraction, such as replying to a text message, checking your e-mail, downloading a song to your iPod, or anything else. If you string together enough of these 15- to 30-minute episodes of writing, eventually you'll have a rough draft. And if you start your assignment early enough, you won't need to panic and try to complete everything minutes before it is due.

It's okay to take breaks. Get up from your computer and stretch. Get something to drink. But don't make the breaks longer than the writing session. If your mind (or heart) isn't into writing, then do something else. But at those times when you are in the mood to write, write! I have to tell you that I'm this way; if I'm not in the mood to write, then I don't do it—I go do something else. But when my brain is in that "writing mode," I try to milk it for all it's worth and get as much done as I can. Before you take a break, though, try to map out what you will be writing about next time you sit down to write. Leave yourself some notes, or a skeleton outline in your file, so that when you come back to it you'll be able to jumpstart yourself and pick up your thoughts.

Save all of your rough drafts (SparkNotes, 2006). As you go through the editing and revising process, you may cut out sentences or even paragraphs, then realize later on that you want to put something back in. If you do all your writing and editing in one file, deleted information is likely to be gone (unless you are using Microsoft Word's "track changes" mode, in which case writing a rough draft would be cumbersome). So name your first rough draft, for example, "term paper draft 1.0," then whenever you make minor revisions, use the "save as" function and rename the next file "draft 1.1," "draft 1.2," and so forth. Whenever I complete a major revision, I bump the revision number up, to "draft 2.0," and so on. This will leave you with a trail of your rough drafts, which is also a nice way to demonstrate the work that you did throughout the writing process.

EDITING YOUR WORK

Editing can occur at multiple times in the writing process. However, editing cannot occur until there is something to edit! Thus, getting anything down for a rough draft, no matter how rough it is, allows you to begin the process of improvement. Many authors provide valuable tips for the editing process, such as placing a ruler under each line as you read it so that your eyes have a manageable amount of text to review (University of Arkansas at Little Rock, 2002). Here are some helpful suggestions and tips for editing from Texas A&M University (2011):

- After you finish your rough draft, set it aside for a period of time before looking at it again. This will allow you to review it with a fresh perspective.
- If you are going to self-edit, double or triple space your draft so you'll have room to write down suggestions.
- Be brutal with yourself; don't settle, and don't take shortcuts. Delete, substitute, rearrange, insert, and create new if you need to.
- Give special consideration to beginning and ending paragraphs.
- Read it out loud. You will hear some mistakes that you didn't see. Just take care to read each word verbatim—our brains autocorrect many of the errors that can occur. Better yet, have someone else read your draft out loud to you.
- Keep a list of your most common errors so that you can improve and learn to avoid those errors in the future.

More editing suggestions are offered by Lipkewich (2001):

- Read your own work backwards. Read the last sentence, then the second-to-last sentence, and so on.
- Does each sentence make sense when you read it on its own?
- Do you see or hear any errors in the sentence?

- Be sure that every sentence has two parts: the subject (who or what) and the predicate (what is happening).
- Use sentence-combining words such as *and, but, or, yet, who, whom, which, that, whose, because, although, when, if, where,* and others.
- Use periods and commas where necessary, but do not overuse them.
- Do not overuse the exclamation point!
- Use a dictionary to check spelling in addition to any software spell-checkers you may use.

REVISING YOUR WORK

You've completed the hard work of creating the best rough draft that you can, and you have sought out editorial comment. You may have self-edited, had a peer edit your work, or perhaps your instructor edited and/or graded your rough draft. Your draft may have been returned to you with some of the symbols presented later in Figure 4.6. With this invaluable feedback, now it's time to revise your work.

Revising is simply looking back at your writing and making changes. What types of changes? You might decide to add new information that you can now see is missing, or you might take out information you now know is unnecessary or tangential to your main topic. You might rearrange the order or sequence of ideas, sentences, or even complete paragraphs to tell a more compelling story, and you might change or substitute words now that you can begin to see the big picture coming together. Revising is *not* proofreading for typographical errors or misplaced words, and just because you used spell-check does not mean that the revision process is complete (Empire State College, n.d.-b). Consider the first draft of a simulated student paper (Figure 4.3). I've created this so it would be a realistic first draft of part of a term paper or literature review that a student might be working on.

Remember, the goal of a first draft is to just get ideas down. Rather than marking up every spelling mistake and instance of incorrect citation style, your instructor may instead give you a list of broader goals for improving your work, expecting you to make the finer corrections yourself. If I were grading this sample paper, I might create a list of revision feedback that listed the following items:

- Focus your first paragraph a little better. First, get rid of the word *thing* because it's too vague. Second, I think readers will agree that hate and hate crimes are painful, so expand on the ways in which hate is real. I'm not sure I get the connection between fast-paced lifestyles, stress, and hate. Anger, yes, but why hate?
- OK, I see what you mean about societal changes leading to hate. Interesting idea that without a stratified class system, we create our own in- and out-groups. What does *introversion* mean?

FIGURE 4.3

Hate is a very real and painful thing in our society today. We gave seen case after case all throughout history where hate crimes have been committed mainly towards groups of minorities. Today's lifestyle is fast paced, stressful and the society has changed. These factors combined cause flared anger and frustrations. These things lead us to the hate that we see displayed today.

In a society that has fundamentally rejected class and caste, each of us looks elsewhere for identifications. The result has been a tendency toward introversions and "in-group" association, the manifestations of which are too often bigotry, prejudice and discrimination against those thought to constitute the "out-group." Tacitly accepted for so long as imply a fact of American life discrimination has now emerged as probably the most significant domestic social issue of our times, and already quite the most violent (Newman 1-2).

Newman points out a problem our society has today. This is a problem that has been created by the society itself, and it is a problem that needs to be handled in a sociological manner. Whillock argues that "hate is not viewed as outside the bounds of societal interest. From societal sanctioning of the Salem witch-hunts or the McCrthy hearings, to outrage over Wounded Knee and Mi Lai, American history is replete with examples of how society has attempted to come to terms with acts of hatred. Such struggles will continue to exist as longs as we keep trying to define (or redefine) our culture's core values and the consequent objects for its disdain (47).

Sample first draft.

- Please clarify: Do you think discrimination is the most significant domestic social issue of our times *because* it has caused the most violence? Is this the way Newman defines its significance? Your citations are not in APA style—please correct.
- Need smoother transition between second and third paragraph. "Newman points out a problem. . . ." Huh? Sounds like you are about to move to a new topic.
- Not clear where Whillock quote begins and ends. Who's cited at end of paragraph 3?

- Like the sentence about Salem witch hunts, etc., and relevance of these examples to the idea that defining values goes hand in hand with defining what is not valued.
- Please proofread. There are a few obvious spelling mistakes.

When you look at the final draft (Figure 4.4), you'll notice that the student took charge of the line edits and proofreading and took some of the suggestions but ignored others. This is typically OK unless you are ignoring a key point that your instructor has been emphasizing. The text becomes a bit shorter, but it reads much better. You may have to go through more than one revision cycle; also, try to have as many people look at it as possible. Have a classmate proofread your work (and offer to proofread his or hers). Have your instructor (if possible) or a teaching

FIGURE 4.4

Hate is a real phenomenon in society today. We see case after case throughout history where hate crimes were committed towards groups of minorities. Today's lifestyle is fast paced, stressful and the society has changed. These complexities combined cause anger, frustration, and the hate we see displayed today.

In a society that has fundamentally rejected class and caste, each of us looks elsewhere for identifications. The result is a tendency toward introversions and "in-group" association; the manifestations of which are bigotry, prejudice, and discrimination. Tacitly accepted for so long as simply a fact of American life, discrimination is now probably the most significant domestic social issue of our time, and already quite violent (Newman, 2002).

Newman states that this problem was created by society, and it is a problem that needs to be addressed from a sociological perspective. Whillock (2003) argues that "hate is not viewed as outside the bounds of societal interest" (p. 492). From societal sanctioning of the Salem witch-hunts or the McCarthy hearings, to outrage over Wounded Knee and Mi Lai, American history is replete with examples of how society has attempted to come to terms with acts of hatred. Such struggles will continue to exist as long as society strives to define (or redefine) our culture's core values and future objects of disdain (Newman, 2002).

Sample first draft, revised.

assistant proofread your work so you have multiple revision opportunities. And remember, you will only have time for this part of the revision process if you finish your drafts a bit ahead of time.

This revision process is common throughout all of scientific writing. In fact, your faculty members who do research and publish know much about revision. Rarely, and I mean rarely, will a scholarly paper be accepted on its first submission to a professional journal. In fact, the outcome that most aspiring scientists hope for is "revise and resubmit." That is, the journal has technically rejected the first submission for publication, but the editorial feedback is for the author to revise his or her work and resubmit it, hoping for an eventual acceptance. The process that faculty members follow with their students, that is, draft–edit–revise, is the exact process that faculty members follow in their professional careers. One of the reasons faculty members invest so much time and effort into grading and marking student papers is because we are modeling the professional practices of our discipline for students.

PROOFREADING YOUR WORK

The last stage in this draft–edit–revise cycle is proofreading. When you think you are about done with your final product, proofreading is the process of making final corrections and changes to your near-finished paper. What types of errors are you looking for at this stage of the process? According to Hibbard (2001), the most common errors identified during proofreading are incorrectly spelled names, reversed numbers, incorrect dates, incorrect or inconsistent capitalization, double-typed words or phrases, omissions of words or parts of words, incorrect or missing punctuation, nonagreement of subject and verb, and misspelled words. Proofreading is not the stage at which you are creating new sections of the paper, and it is not the stage at which major changes are made—that should have been accomplished during the revision process. Proofreading is the "fine tuning" that occurs before that wonderful feeling of being finished with a quality product.

Numerous authors have offered numerous suggestions to facilitate successful proofreading. Taking the suggestions of Hibbard (2001), Texas A&M University (2011), the University of Arkansas at Little Rock (2002), and the University of North Carolina at Chapel Hill (n.d.), I created the checklist in Exhibit 4.2 as a guide to proofreading.

Finally, and this suggestion was made previously regarding the rough draft–revision process, read every word out loud, or better yet, have someone else read every word out loud to you. This will help you to determine whether you've left little words out or put extra words in (Szuchman, 2005).

EXHIBIT 4.2

Proofreading Checklist

Check (✓) one

Yes	No	Proofreading Questions to Consider
___	___	Did you proofread from a printed copy (not from the computer screen)?
___	___	Did you look for words that are commonly misused? (A list of these is presented in Exhibit 4.5.)
___	___	Did you allow some time to pass between finishing the last revision and your final proofreading?
___	___	Did you proofread one last time before you printed your final copy or sent the final copy?
___	___	Are there both open and closed quotation marks and parentheses?
___	___	Is the punctuation spaced consistently?
___	___	Is there too much or too little space anywhere in the final draft?
___	___	Have all the names and dates been checked and double checked?
___	___	Are all the bullets aligned?
___	___	Are all the word divisions (hyphenations) correct?
___	___	Have you used spell-check and grammar-check?
___	___	Did you proofread for one type of error at a time?
___	___	Did you read slowly and read every word?
___	___	Did you circle every punctuation mark to ensure every sentence ended with a punctuation mark?

How to Avoid Plagiarism With Style and Good Academic Citizenship

What is plagiarism? According to Landau (2003, para. 3), "Plagiarism occurs when people take credit for thoughts, words, images, musical passages, or ideas originally created by someone else." The Council of Writing Program Administrators (2003, para. 4) defined plagiarism as "when a writer deliberately uses someone else's language, ideas, or other original (not common-knowledge) material without acknowledging its source." Essentially, plagiarism is the failure to give credit where credit is due. There are serious consequences for students who are caught plagiarizing; these vary from instructor to instructor as well as from institution to institution. You should be able to find detailed information about this in your student handbook. The consequences could be receiving an F on the assignment, an F in the course, and, in some cases, worse. In the real world, plagiarism has its consequences, too:

> Less than two weeks after he was called to task for borrowing liberally from others in his welcome address to the freshman

class, the president of Hamilton College resigned on Tuesday. Although some faculty members had criticized Eugene M. Tobin, many people on the campus expressed surprise and disappointment at his resignation. Mr. Tobin stepped down after nine years at the helm of the Clinton, NY, college. He spoke to his colleagues at an afternoon faculty meeting after having consulted with a circle of advisors and constituents almost continuously from the time his act of plagiarism was exposed last month. In a convocation address that focused on the books he had read over the summer, Mr. Tobin used phrases and passages, without citation, from a number of book reviews and descriptions posted on Amazon.com. (Margulies, 2002, paras. 1–2, 4).

This is not the only example of a college president losing his job— plagiarism is not acceptable at any level of higher education.

Harris (2005) and Landau (2003) suggested two main types of plagiarism—intentional and unintentional. Intentional plagiarism is a purposeful act in which deception on the part of the writer is premeditated. Exhibit 4.3 from Harris (2005) presents examples of what most would consider acts of intentional plagiarism. Unintentional plagiarism occurs when there is no intent to plagiarize, yet it happens anyway. This may be due to a lack of knowledge about proper citation rules, carelessness, inappropriate use of a source, or other unintended actions (Council of Writing Program Administrators, 2003; Harris, 2005).

Sometimes it is difficult to differentiate between plagiarism and sloppy citation style, which emphasizes the importance of your instructors teaching you about proper citations (in our case, APA style) and how to avoid plagiarism. Let me present you with some of these "sticky situations" and practice a bit with determining whether the writing constitutes plagiarism or the misuse of sources. The idea for this exercise comes from Shadle (2006), but the actual source material is cited in the box below. Here is the original text from Price (2002), with the proper APA reference:

EXHIBIT 4.3

Examples of Intentional Plagiarism

- Downloading and turning in a paper from the Web, including a Web page or paper mill essay
- Copying and pasting phrases, sentences, or paragraphs into your paper without showing a quotation or adding the proper citation
- Paraphrasing or summarizing a source's words or ideas without proper citation
- Including a graph, table, or picture from a source without proper citation
- Getting so much help from a tutor or writing helper that the paper or part of the paper is no longer honestly your work
- Turning in previously written work when that practice is prohibited by your instructor

But plagiarism is not stable. What we think of as plagiarism shifts across historical time periods, across cultures, across workplaces, even across academic disciplines. We need to stop treating plagiarism like a pure moral absolute ("Thou shalt not plagiarize") and start explaining it in a way that accounts for these shifting features of contexts.

Price, M. (2002). Beyond "gotcha!": Situating plagiarism in policy and pedagogy. *College Composition and Communication, 54,* 88–115. doi:10.2307/1512103

If you were going to use that as a direct quote in your APA-style paper, here is what it would look like (note that the text is indented because the quote is longer than 40 words):

But plagiarism is not stable. What we think of as plagiarism shifts across historical time periods, across cultures, across workplaces, even across academic disciplines. We need to stop treating plagiarism like a pure moral absolute ("Thou shalt not plagiarize") and start explaining it in a way that accounts for these shifting features of contexts. (Price, 2002, p. 90)

But what if a student were to write a paragraph in his or her paper exactly like the one below—would this be plagiarism?

Plagiarism is very difficult to understand because it is not stable. What we think of as plagiarism shifts across historical time periods, across cultures, across workplaces, even across academic disciplines. We need to stop treating plagiarism like a pure moral absolute and start explaining it in a way that accounts for these shifting features of contexts.

For most faculty, the answer would be yes, this is plagiarism. Not only are most of the phrases identical to the original, but there is absolutely no attribution to the author (remember, we must give credit where credit is due). If I were to read a paragraph like this in a student's paper, I would have to assume that this idea was the student's original idea because of the lack of attribution.

The example above is fairly blatant, but what about this one?

According to Price, plagiarism is not stable. What we think of as plagiarism shifts across historical time periods, across cultures, across workplaces, even across academic disciplines. We need to stop treating plagiarism like a pure moral absolute and start explaining it in a way that accounts for these shifting features of contexts ("Beyond 'Gotcha,'" p. 90).

I would consider this example either unintentional plagiarism or just using a sloppy citation method. It does give credit where credit is due, which is good. However, after the first sentence almost everything else is a direct quote, and thus should be presented as a direct quote.

Also—and I have to tell you this drives me up a wall—this example uses Modern Language Association citation style, not APA. Make sure you follow the style that your instructor wants, not a style you may have previously learned in another class!

WHAT ARE THE CAUSES OF PLAGIARISM?

Whether intentional or not, there really is no excuse for plagiarism at any level. However, it does happen, and understanding the causes of plagiarism can help you develop strategies to avoid plagiarism. Students are motivated to plagiarize for a number of reasons: Some may fear failure or taking risks in writing; others may have inadequate time management skills and think they have no choice but to plagiarize. Other students may believe that the assignment, course, or rules of APA style and format are unimportant or that the consequences of plagiarism are unimportant or rarely enforced.

To be honest, teachers can be part of the problem as well—some of the causes of plagiarism are linked to the lack of instruction and consistency from faculty members. Instructors need to design writing assignments to minimize the risk or threat of plagiarism (more on this later). Teachers may create assignments that are so generic or like busywork that students feel completing them is a waste of their time, thereby justifying (in students' minds) cheating. Also, teachers and institutions may not consistently report plagiarism when it occurs, penalize it appropriately, or track it over time (Council of Writing Program Administrators, 2003).

HOW TO AVOID PLAGIARISM

Students and faculty members need to share in the responsibility of taking steps to prevent plagiarism. As a student, you are responsible for your part of this bargain, but know that faculty must also hold up their end of the bargain. Students need to (a) understand that intentional plagiarism harms their character, (b) know that intentional plagiarism cheats themselves, and (c) know that plagiarism is not a practice that is accepted as a trait of a well-rounded, educated citizen. Faculty members need to demonstrate APA format and style in the use of Web-based materials, and they need to talk about the underlying implications of plagiarism and what it might mean for a student's future. Faculty members also need to design writing assignments in such a way that the potential for plagiarism is minimized (such as reviewing students' article summaries, reviewing rough drafts of student work, examining reference and idea notecards used in writing, etc.), and they need to include in their syllabuses the course and university policies on plagiarism (Council of Writing Program Administrators, 2003; Harris, 2005; University of Maryland University College, 2005b).

PROTECTING YOURSELF FROM PLAGIARISM

There are strategies that you should follow that will help you avoid a charge of plagiarism. The strategies in Exhibit 4.4 come from Harris (2005), and they are excellent suggestions for protecting yourself from plagiarism.

Unfortunately, if an instructor has been teaching long enough, he or she has encountered cheating, including plagiarism, in some form or another. I tell you the following story to demonstrate how important attitude can be, and the good that can come from being honest. I once caught two students in an upper division psychology class cheating (it wasn't plagiarism, but copying an assignment). To be honest, intent is sometimes hard to determine even when the instance of cheating is not hard to detect (one student had completed a homework assignment and copied it, and each student put his/her name on a separate copy). I confronted both students with my discovery. I told them that this was cheating and an act of academic dishonesty and that there would be punishment. One student was extremely apologetic, and after thinking about it, realized what he/she had done and eventually apologized for it. The other student was offended that he/she had been called a cheater and expressed no responsibility or remorse for his/her actions. The former student went on to do great things in our department and was quite successful. The latter student seemed to just fade away into the woodwork. The point of my story is this: How you deal with conditions that tempt you to plagiarize, and your maturity in accepting responsibility for your actions, can make a big difference in how you are perceived by others and the future opportunities you may be afforded. Own your mistakes!

EXHIBIT 4.4

Plagiarism Avoidance: Avoid Being a Victim, Avoid Being Charged With Plagiarism

1. Protect your data and your computer passwords to protect against theft.
2. Do not lend, give, or upload any paper to anyone, even if a student just wants to see what an APA-formatted paper looks like.
3. Report any theft immediately, including to the proper authorities and, in the case of your academic work, your instructors.
4. Save and print all drafts and notes—having your reference and idea notecards will help support the originality of your written work.
5. Photocopy or print all of your sources, and do not cite something that you have not actually read yourself.
6. Be proactive in seeking out the advice of your instructor and teaching assistants. If someone has been reviewing your work all semester, it will be easier for you to make the case that your work is actually your work.

Plagiarism is a form of cheating with serious consequences. I agree with Harris's (2005) statement that "the goal of education is not to get through, but to get better" (p. 15). If you intend to cheat your way through college, why bother? I've been saying to my students for years, would you want to go to the hospital for surgery with a physician who had cheated his or her way through medical school? Would you want to consult a lawyer who had cheated through law school, or a therapist who had cheated through graduate school? Plagiarism and cheating have the potential to be harmful to others, but most of all they are harmful to you.

Quiz Yourself on APA Style

Because I am not a grammarian, I rely on the advice of others to provide useful tips for avoiding common writing mistakes. There are many good resources available to help you avoid common mistakes (e.g., Bellquist, 1993; Shertzer, 1986). Some are classics, like *The Elements of Style* (Strunk & White, 1979), and there are many updated versions in standalone books, in English books, and on the Internet. In chapters 5 and 6, I present specific instructions and examples of APA style and format for scientific writing assignments. In this section, I provide numerous helpful resource materials that you may want to refer to frequently when writing and revising your written work. Figure 4.5 contains an example of an exercise from Freimuth (2008) used to help identify APA errors. There are many different types of errors. See how many you can find, and then check your work against the errors I found (my marked-up version of this exercise appears at the end of the chapter in Figure 4.8).

When an instructor is editing your work (as in my marked-up version at the end of this chapter), he or she may choose to use editing marks rather than writing out comments individually (this saves time). Some editing marks are fairly universal, and some examples are provided in Figure 4.6 (Merriam-Webster, 2007).

Although the marks in Figure 4.6 are useful, it makes more sense to show you how they work in actual student work. In chapters 5 and 6, I present some sample rough drafts of actual student work and show you how I would actually mark that work if I were grading it (the students' final drafts are also included). Of course, instructors don't always put every comment they want to on student work because (one hopes) most instructors want to encourage students to work to see improvements in writing and the critical thinking that accompanies it. But just for fun, Figure 4.7 displays some sample editing marks that would be entertaining to see sometimes.

FIGURE 4.5

SELF-SCORING EXERCISE   1

Discussion

This study investigated the relationships among stress, personality type, anger and chronic disease. Two of the four hypotheses, discussed previously, were found to be true. Consistent with the work of Garon and Mantel (2003), the correlation between stress level and disease was very significant. However, its worth noting that the affect of personality type was statistically insignificant. The lack of relationship between personality and chronic disease is inconsistent with previous studies (Harrison et al., 2006; Davis, Wolf and Jones, 2004). The ANOVA that compares high- and low-anger participants yielded the most significant finding (p = .001). The data was consistent with previous research showing that anger effected stress level (Harrison, Holstein, Calf, Grobeck, & Nelson, 2006). Higher levels of reported anger were associated with significantly less stress. These findings have important implications for health psychologists. Facilitating a person's expression of anger can reduce stress and lower their risk for disease.

Two of the desired inclusion criterion for the participant sample were not met. The vast majority of subjects were Caucasian. Orientals, Mexican-Americans, and blacks accounted for only 9% of the sample. Also, there were too few female participants; there were twenty-five women and two hundred men. Thus, the data could not be used to examine whether gender or ethnicity impacted risk for disease.

This study extends the work of Parlick & Wilson (2007) whose research the American Psychosomatic Society (as cited in Parlick & Wilson, 2007) recently honored as "cutting edge in the field". They argue, "The progress made in late 20th century stress research has exceeded expectations. Our rapidly growing understanding of psychological factors, in the development and treatment of chronic disease, has set the stage for major breakthroughs in health psychology (p. 195)."

Sample assignment in need of APA format. From *A Self-Scoring Exercise on APA Style and Research Language* (p. 5), by M. Freimuth, 2008, Santa Barbara, CA: The Fielding Graduate University. Copyright 2008 by Marilyn Freimuth. Adapted with permission.

FIGURE 4.5 (Continued)

SELF-SCORING EXERCISE   2

Bibliography

Davis, T., Wolf, M., & Jones, F. (2004). Disease and personality. *Psychological Summaries, 45*,

45-67.

Garon, D. and Mantel, J. (2003). Stress and disease. In M. Wilson (Ed.), *Psychology of Disease*

(p. 12-38). Boston, MA: Po Press.

Harrison, B. T., Holstein, C., Calf, F. T., Grobeck, A., & Nelson, F. V. (2006). Introversion-

extroversion predicts disease states [Electronic version].

Psychological Summaries, 43(4), 257-289. Retrieved, December 8, 2007 from

http:/healthcareusa.com.htm

Parlick, T., & Wilson, M. (2007). *Health and Mind.* Paris, France: Dix.

Sample assignment in need of APA format. From *A Self-Scoring Exercise on APA Style and Research Language* (p. 6), by M. Freimuth, 2008, Santa Barbara, CA: The Fielding Graduate University. Copyright 2008 by Marilyn Freimuth. Adapted with permission.

Table 4.3 includes a listing of the 20 most common errors that occur in student essays (other than misspellings). In this listing based on Connors and Lunsford (1988, as cited in Gottschalk & Hjortshoj, 2004; see also Lunsford, n.d.), I provide the error and an example that demonstrates the error. Remember, this is what NOT to do!

As I mentioned earlier, there are many good resources that present detailed information about common mistakes and how to avoid them. Exhibits 4.5 and 4.6 present commonly confused words and commonly misspelled words; information for both tables comes from Scott, Koch, Scott, and Garrison (2002).

Although there are over 90 different reference formats presented in the *APA Publication Manual,* the following examples are from the most common sources that you are likely to cite. Here I provide some examples of different types of reference material prepared in APA format. Citing electronic documents can be particularly tricky. I suggest you consult the *APA Style Guide to Electronic References* (APA, 2012a). This is actually a PDF available for purchase at http://www.apa.org/pubs/books.

FIGURE 4.6

Symbol	Meaning	Example
ℰ or ℽ or ℴℐ	delete	take it out
◌	close up	print as o ne word
ℰ̃	delete and close up	close up
∧ or > or ∧	caret	insert here ⌐something
#	insert a space	put onehere
eq#	space evenly	space evenly ∧ where indicated
stet	let stand	let marked tout stand as set
tr	transpose	change order the
/	used to separate two or more marks and often as a concluding stroke at the end of an insertion	
⌐	set farther to the left	L too far to the right
⌐	set farther to the right	too⌐ far to the left
⌒	set as ligature (such as æ)	encyclopaedia
=	align horizontally	alignment
‖	align vertically	‖ align with surrounding text
x	broken character	imperfect
▯	indent or insert em quad space	
¶	begin a new paragraph	
⑤ℙ	spell out	set 5 lbs. as five pounds
cap	set in CAPITALS	set nato as NATO
sm cap or s.c.	set in SMALL CAPITALS	set signal as SIGNAL
lc	set in lowercase	set South as south
ital	set in *italic*	set oeuvre as *oeuvre*
rom	set in roman	set mensch as mensch
bf	set in **boldface**	set important as **important**
= or -/ or ≅ or /ᴴ/	hyphen	multi-colored
$\frac{1}{N}$ or en or /ℕ/	en dash	1965–72
$\frac{1}{M}$ or em or /ℳ/	em (or long) dash	Now—at last!—we know.
∨	superscript or superior	∛as in πr^2
∧	subscript or inferior	∧ as in H_2O
◇ or ✕	centered	◇ for a centered dot in $p \cdot q$
⌐	comma	
∨	apostrophe	
⊙	period	
; or ;/	semicolon	
: or ⊙	colon	
⌣⌣ or ⌣⌣	quotation marks	

Common proofreading marks. From Proofreaders' Marks. Retrieved from http://www.m-w.com/mw/table/proofrea.htm. Copyright 2007 by Merriam-Webster. Reprinted with permission.

FIGURE 4.7

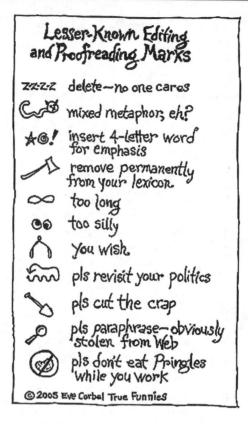

Much-needed proofreading marks. From *Lesser-Known Editing and Proof-reading Marks.* © Eve Corbel, trufunnies.ca. Reprinted with permission.

PERIODICAL OR JOURNAL ARTICLE

Blanton, P. G. (2001). A model of supervising undergraduate internships. *Teaching of Psychology, 28,* 217–219.

Kampfe, C. M., Mitchell, M. M., Boyless, J. A., & Sauers, G. O. (1999). Undergraduate students' perceptions of the internship: An exploratory study. *Rehabilitation Education, 13,* 359–367.

McGovern, T. V., Furumoto, L., Halpern, D. F., Kimble, G. A., & McKeachie, W. J. (1991). Liberal education, study in depth, and the arts and sciences major—Psychology. *American Psychologist, 46,* 598–605.

TABLE 4.3

Grammatical Problems to Avoid

Twenty most common errors	Example of the error
1. No comma after an introductory element	Well it wasn't really true.
2. Vague pronoun reference	John told his father that his car had been stolen.
3. No comma in compound sentence	I like to eat but I hate to gain weight.
4. Wrong word	His F in math enhanced his alarm about his D in chemistry.
5. Missing comma(s) with a nonrestrictive element	The students who had unsuccessfully concealed their participation in the prank were expelled.
6. Wrong or missing verb ending	I use to go often to town.
7. Wrong or missing preposition	Cottonwood Grille is located at Boise.
8. Comma splice	Chloe liked the cat, however, she was allergic to it.
9. Missing or misplaced possessive apostrophe	Student's backpacks weigh far too much.
10. Unnecessary shift in tense	I was happily watching TV when suddenly my sister attacks me.
11. Unnecessary shift in pronoun	When one is tired, you should sleep.
12. Sentence fragment	He went shopping in the local sports store. An outing he usually enjoyed. [The second part is the fragment.]
13. Wrong tense or verb form	I would not have said that if I thought it would have shocked her.
14. Lack of subject–verb agreement.	Having many close friends, especially if you've known them for a long time, are a great help in times of trouble.
15. Missing comma in a series	Students eat, sleep and do homework.
16. Lack of agreement between pronoun and antecedent	When someone plagiarizes from material on a Web site, they are likely to be caught.
17. Unnecessary comma(s) with a restrictive element	The novel, that my teacher assigned, was very boring.
18. Run-on or fused sentence	He loved the seminar he even loved the readings.
19. Dangling or misplaced modifier	After being put to sleep, a small incision is made below the navel.
20. *Its–it's* confusion.	Its a splendid data for everyone.

Note. The examples in the table are (mostly) from Gottschalk and Hjortshoj (2004).

EXHIBIT 4.5

Commonly Confused Words

advice/advise	conscience/conscious	hear/here	passed/past
affect/effect	corps/corpse	heard/herd	patience/patients
aisle/isle	council/counsel	hole/whole	peace/piece
allusion/illusion	dairy/diary	human/humane	personal/personnel
an/and	desert/dessert	its/it's	plain/plane
angel/angle	device/devise	know/no	precede/proceed
ascent/assent	die/dye	later/latter	presence/presents
bare/bear	dominant/dominate	lay/lie	principal/principle
brake/break	elicit/illicit	lead/led	quiet/quite
breath/breathe	eminent/immanent/im	lessen/lesson	rain/reign/rein
buy/by	minent	loose/lose	raise/raze
capital/capitol	envelop/envelope	may	reality/realty
choose/chose	every day/everyday	be/maybe	respectfully/
cite/sight/site	fair/fare	miner/minor	respectively
complement/	formally/formerly	moral/morale	reverend/reverent
compliment	forth/fourth	of/off	

Note. From *The Psychology Student Writer's Manual* (2nd ed., pp. 52–54), by J. M. Scott, R. Koch, G. M. Scott, and S. M. Garrison, 2002, Upper Saddle River, NJ: Pearson Education. Copyright 2002 by Pearson Education. Reprinted with permission.

BOOK

Chickering, A. W., & Reisser, L. (1993). *Education and identity* (2nd ed.). San Francisco: Jossey-Bass.

Council of Graduate Schools. (1989). *Why graduate school?* Washington, DC: Author.

Jones, R. A. (1985). *Research methods in the social and behavioral sciences.* Sunderland, MA: Sinauer Associates.

EDITED BOOK

Chastain, G., & Landrum, R. E. (Eds.). (1999). *Protecting human subjects: Departmental subject pools and institutional review boards.* Washington, DC: American Psychological Association.

CHAPTER IN EDITED BOOK

Crawford, M. P. (1992). Rapid growth and change at the American Psychological Association: 1945 to 1970. In R. B. Evans, V. S. Sexton, & T. C. Cadwallader (Eds.), *The American Psychological Association: A historical perspective* (pp. 177–232). Washington, DC: American Psychological Association.

EXHIBIT 4.6

Commonly Misspelled Words

a lot	experience	nuisance	satellite
acceptable	fascinate	occasion	scarcity
accessible	finally	occasionally	scenery
accommodate	foresee	occurred	science
accompany	forty	occurrences	secede
accustomed	fulfill	omission	secession
acquire	gauge	omit	secretary
against	guaranteed	opinion	senseless
annihilate	guard	opponent	separate
apparent	harass	parallel	sergeant
arguing	hero	parole	shining
argument	heroes	peaceable	significant
authentic	humorous	performance	sincerely
before	hurried	pertain	skiing
begin	hurriedly	practical	stubbornness
beginning	hypocrite	preparation	studying
believe	ideally	probably	succeed
benefited	immediately	process	success
bulletin	immense	professor	successfully
business	incredible	prominent	susceptible
cannot	innocuous	pronunciation	suspicious
category	intercede	psychology	technical
committee	interrupt	publicly	temporary
condemn	irrelevant	pursue	tendency
courteous	irresistible	pursuing	therefore
definitely	irritate	questionnaire	tragedy
dependent	knowledge	realize	truly
desperate	license	receipt	tyranny
develop	likelihood	received	unanimous
different	maintenance	recession	unconscious
disappear	manageable	recommend	undoubtedly
disappoint	meanness	referring	until
easily	mischievous	religious	vacuum
efficient	missile	remembrance	valuable
environment	necessary	reminisce	various
equipped	nevertheless	repetition	vegetable
exceed	no one	representative	visible
exercise	noticeable	rhythm	without
existence	noticing	ridiculous	women
		roommate	writing

Note. From *The Psychology Student Writer's Manual* (2nd ed., pp. 52–54), by J. M. Scott, R. Koch, G. M. Scott, and S. M. Garrison, 2002, Upper Saddle River, NJ: Pearson Education. Copyright 2002 by Pearson Education. Reprinted with permission.

Lord, C. G. (2004). A guide to PhD graduate school: How they keep score in the big leagues. In J. M. Darley, M. P. Zanna, & H. L. Roediger III (Eds.), *The compleat academic: A career guide* (2nd ed., pp. 3–15). Washington, DC: American Psychological Association.

CONFERENCE PRESENTATION

Appleby, D. (1999, April). *Advice and strategies for job-seeking psychology majors.* Paper presented at the annual meeting of the Midwestern Psychological Association, Chicago.

Kennedy, J. H., & Lloyd, M. A. (1998, August). *Effectiveness of a Careers in Psychology course for majors.* Poster presented at the 107th Annual Convention of the American Psychological Association, San Francisco.

MAGAZINE ARTICLE

Buskist, W. (2002, Spring). Seven tips for preparing a successful application to graduate school in psychology. *Eye on Psi Chi, 5*(3), 32–34.

Kanchier, C. (2002, April 12–14). Does your attitude limit your options? *USA Weekend Magazine*, p. 9.

OTHER MATERIALS

Educational Testing Service. (2001). *Coming in October 2002: A new GRE general test* [Brochure]. Princeton, NJ: Author.

Landrum, R. E., Taki, R., & Bushee, L. L. (2006). *The challenge of using survey data to help determine elementary school policies.* (ERIC Document Reproduction Service No. ED490 795).

INTERNET MATERIALS

Hopper, C. (1998). *Ten tips you need to survive college.* Retrieved from http://www.mtsu.edu/~studskl/10tips.html

Landau, J. D. (2003). *Understanding and preventing plagiarism.* Retrieved from http://www.psychologicalscience.org/teaching/tips/tips_0403.html

Lloyd, M. A. (1997, August 28). *Exploring career-related abilities, interests, skills, and values.* Retrieved from http://www.psychweb.com/careers/explore.htm

Figure 4.8 presents my marked-up copy of the Discussion previously presented. Your instructor may not be as picky as I am, or perhaps he or she will be more picky. In other words, write for your instructor, because each person has specific likes and dislikes, and as much as we try to objectify the grading of written work, it is very much a subjective process.

FIGURE 4.8

SELF-SCORING EXERCISE   1

A study does not investigate - researchers do.

Discussion

This (study investigated) the relationships among stress, personality type, anger and

chronic disease. Two of the four hypotheses, discussed previously, were ~~found to be true.~~ *supported*

Consistent with the work of Garon and Mantel (2003), the correlation between stress level and

disease was ~~very~~ significant. However, its worth noting that the *e*ffect of personality type was

statistically insignificant. The lack of relationship between personality and chronic disease is

inconsistent with previous studies [Harrison et al., 2006; Davis, Wolf, ~~and~~ Jones, 2004]. ~~The~~ *I used an*

ANOVA ~~that~~ *to* compare*d* high- and low-anger participants *which* yielded ~~the most~~ *a* significant finding (*p*

were = .001). The data ~~was~~ consistent with previous research showing that anger *a*ffected stress level

et al. (Harrison, ~~Holstein, Calf, Grobeck, & Nelson~~, 2006). Higher levels of reported anger were

double-check this - The higher the anger, the less the stress?

associated with significantly less stress. These findings have important implications for health

psychologists. Facilitating a person's expression of anger can reduce stress and lower their risk

for disease.

    Two of the desired inclusion criterion for the participant sample were not met. The vast

participants *People who were Asian, Hispanic, and African-American* majority of ~~subjects~~ were Caucasian. ~~Orientals, Mexican-Americans, and blacks~~ accounted for

25 only 9% of the sample. Also, there were too few female participants; there were ~~twenty-five~~

200 women and ~~two hundred~~ men. Thus, the data could not be used to examine whether gender or

the ethnicity impacted risk for disease.

    This study extends the work of Parlick *and* ~~&~~ Wilson (2007) whose research ~~the American~~ *was*

~~Psychosomatic Society (as cited in Parlick & Wilson, 2007)~~ recently honored as "cutting edge in

the field. They argue, "The progress made in late 20th century stress research has exceeded

expectations. Our rapidly growing understanding of psychological factors, in the development

and treatment of chronic disease, has set the stage for major breakthroughs in health psychology

(p. 195)."

Sample paper sections with sample instructor marks. From *A Self-Scoring Exercise on APA Style and Research Language* (p. 5), by M. Freimuth, 2008, Santa Barbara, CA: The Fielding Graduate University. Copyright 2008 by Marilyn Freimuth. Adapted with permission.

FIGURE 4.8 (*Continued*)

SELF-SCORING EXERCISE   2

References

~~Bibliography~~

Davis, T., Wolf, M., & Jones, F. (2004). Disease and personality. *Psychological Summaries, 45,*

45-67.

Garon, D., and Mantel, J. (2003). Stress and disease. In M. Wilson (Ed.), *Psychology of Disease*

pp. (p. 12-38). Boston, MA: Po Press.

Harrison, B. T., Holstein, C., Calf, F. T., Grobeck, A., & Nelson, F. V. (2006). Introversion-

extroversion predicts disease states [Electronic version]. —> *Incomplete — need complete retrieval information.*

Psychological Summaries, 43(4), 257-289. Retrieved, December 8, 2007 from *was this electronically retrieved, or paper copy only?*

http:/healthcareusa.com.htm

Author?
Year published?

Parlick, T., & Wilson, M. (2007). *Health and Mind.* Paris, France: Dix.

lower case

Sample paper sections with sample instructor marks. From *A Self-Scoring Exercise on APA Style and Research Language* (p. 6), by M. Freimuth, 2008, Santa Barbara, CA: The Fielding Graduate University. Copyright 2008 by Marilyn Freimuth. Adapted with permission.

Bringing the Audience Up to Speed With Literature Reviews 5

Perfect Term Papers provides a solution to this very problem faced by students overburdened with term papers, essays and book reports. We write highest quality custom term papers, essays and book reports at the Lowest Price available on the Web. The best part about our term papers, research papers, essays and book reports is that they are all original and custom-written exactly according to your specifications! Perfect Term Papers (a) writes non-plagiarized term papers checked in anti-plagiarism software; (b) has the latest references that can be cross checked for authenticity; (c) are sent within the due date; (d) will not be found online; (e) will have 250 words per page; and (f) will have Bibliography pages free.

We do things that others only promise. No more screwed up social lives. No more pains and frustrations over a demanding deadline. No more rejected term papers because of insufficient data, inadequate research or ineffective writing style. Trust us with your problems and let us help you. All you have to do is order your custom term paper and we'll take care of the rest.

Disclaimer: These papers are to be used for research purposes only. Use of these papers for any other purpose is not the responsibility of Perfect Term Papers.

—http://www.perfecttermpapers.com,
retrieved February 20, 2007

T he last chapter ended with information about plagiarism and how to avoid it. From the information above, you can see that much "help" exists on the Internet for writing term papers. However, I highly recommend against using this type of help. Although these types of Web sites do warn in small print not to represent their work as your own, that is a temptation hard to resist. Also, when someone else is preparing original work for you, you are not learning how to become a scientist and a psychologist. You need the skills and abilities to be able to research a paper, make notecards, draw conclusions, analyze and synthesize, and so forth. Writing assignments are precisely designed to aid in the development of all those skills, not merely to create a written product. In this chapter, I discuss literature reviews and term papers.

Literature Reviews Provide Story Context

The *literature* is a fairly generic term that can be used in a number of contexts. First, a student could write a literature review (or lit review, or review of the literature). This entails an integrated synopsis or summary of some aspect of the psychological literature related to a variable or behavior of interest. In addition, the literature review is often a key component of the Introduction portion of a research paper or a lab report. Furthermore, depending on the type of assignment, a review of the literature could be a key component of a term paper. Given the importance of reviewing the literature and the many variations of it that appear in scientific writing, it is worthwhile to spend some time discussing how to write a literature review.

A literature review is meant to do just that—review the existing literature relevant to the topic you are studying. A review article is intended to be a comprehensive review of the published literature in a particular area.

> Review articles are valuable, not only because they cite all the important research in the area surveyed, but also because they compare and evaluate all the key theories in a particular area of research. Again, notice the companion goals of a literature review: to describe and evaluate. (University of Washington, 2005, para. 7)

Eisenberg (2000) described four common types of review articles—those that (a) generate new knowledge, (b) test a theory, (c) integrate theories, and (d) develop and evaluate a new theory.

However, a more common type of literature review is one that is embedded in a larger paper, such as a research paper. A literature review accomplishes much more than just summarizing the literature (Warburton, 2005); for instance, a literature review provides a historical overview of the topic, presents earlier theories, and also provides background on the purpose of the review (i.e., point of view). A well-written literature review helps the reader understand disagreements and debates about the topic in context and also identifies gaps and omissions in previous work or identifies unanswered questions. Finally, a literature review highlights exemplary or seminal studies in a research area, identifies patterns or trends in the literature, and—very important for students—demonstrates the knowledge and skill of the person writing the review. This chapter describes the process of reviewing the literature, which requires the writer to integrate all the scientific writing concepts and skills mentioned so far.

Guiding Principles for Writing Literature Reviews

Galvan (2006) offered a comprehensive set of writing instructions for literature reviews. You begin by identifying the broad problem area (landfills are filling at an exponential rate), but avoid global statements (recycling is important). Early in the review, indicate why the topic being reviewed is important—if you don't convince the reader that the topic is important, then why should he or she bother reading the review? Distinguish between research findings (such as journal articles) and other sources of information (e.g., the opinions of politicians or popular media reports), and be sure to identify a classic or landmark study as such. Sometimes you'll hear these types of studies referred to as *seminal studies,* and the ability to point this out makes you a savvy researcher. You also provide a great service to your reader when you can identify why a particular study is important.

If you are commenting on the timeliness of a topic, you will want to be specific in describing the time frame; this gives the reader some context and explains why it is an important detail. If there are other literature reviews relevant to your topic, be sure to mention them, even if you are not discussing those other reviews in detail. Be careful about making statements such as "No studies have ever been conducted on this topic." You cannot be certain of that statement—many studies have been conducted by researchers and never been published, and a major reason for nonpublication is that no significant results were found. What would be better to say is this: "To my knowledge, there are no published studies available on this topic."

Avoid long lists of nonspecific references. Sometimes students (and experienced researchers) want to either (a) show off their scholarly work by referencing every study they reviewed, whether it is relevant or not, or (b) want to conserve space by citing multiple studies at the end of a sentence or paragraph. There is no magic number of studies that should be cited in a literature review—the goal is to provide a thorough overview of the topic being studied, and that could require any number of studies. If the results of previous studies are inconsistent or vary widely, cite them separately. This actually helps lay the foundation for the later parts of your Introduction section, in which you describe a conflict or gap in the literature, that is, an unresolved question to be answered. Pointing out inconsistencies in the literature helps you to emphasize the need for your study.

Reassembling Pieces of the Story: Synthesis

The analysis, synthesis, and evaluation components of the literature review are all key. Using the notecard method, you will have already analyzed each of the articles you think should be included in your review. That analysis is important, but not enough. You must then synthesize the main ideas presented in the literature with a critical, evaluative viewpoint. This is a skill that everyone has to work at to acquire, and, just like any skill, it takes time and practice.

My colleague Dr. Celia Reaves at Monroe Community College created two samples of a literature review (Reaves, 2004). In Figure 5.1, analysis and extraction has been completed, but the product looks more like a book report than an integrated review of the literature. (Note that all of the citations and authors in this figure and Figure 5.2 are fabricated.) It looks as if the author picked up a stack of idea notecards from each source and wrote an individual paragraph about each. Although analysis is present, there is no synthesis. Synthesis means that you seek out underlying themes and see connections across studies, not just analyze differences between studies. Figure 5.2 shows a much better literature review (Reaves, 2004). Notice that the text is much shorter, and also notice how references about a particular theme have been grouped together. The intellectual benefit of a well-written literature review is that the author has completed this complex task of analysis–synthesis–evaluation for you and thus provided a rich context for understanding the complexity of a particular psychological idea.

FIGURE 5.1

Weinburger (1997) did a study on the benefits of giving Ritalin to very young children. One of the results was that these children made friends more easily, and got along better in the classroom. Weinburger studied 50 children diagnosed with ADHA in a variety of preschool settings.

Franklin (1998) wrote a paper expressing her concerns about using stimulant medications on very young children. She says the long-term effects of these drugs haven't been studied in children that young. She says, "We are giving powerful drugs to children whose nervous systems are not developed yet. We don't know what can happen" (p. 32).

Another researcher (Jones, 1998) pointed out some advantages of using the medications. He says that the children are more compliant, which means that they go along with what the class is doing and the teacher likes them better.

According to Noloko (1999), when very young children with ADHD are given Ritalin, they are less likely to be asked to leave their daycare or preschool setting. This not only makes life easier for their parents, it also allows them the opportunity to interact successfully with other children.

Andrews (1999) pointed out in an article that the FDA has never given its approval to use stimulant medication for very young patients. This is because there is not enough evidence that they are free of long-term complications.

Two researchers (Ngau & Mostomi, 1999) also conducted a study in a variety of day care and preschool settings. They found similar results, showing that teachers were less likely to ask that ADHD children be taken out of the setting if they took Ritalin or other stimulant medications.

Sample literature review without synthesis. From *Teaching APA Style to Beginners* (p. 5), by C. Reaves, 2004. Copyright 2004 by Celia Reaves. Reprinted with permission.

FIGURE 5.1 *(Continued)*

Smith (2000) did another study showing that children with ADHD who took medication were more likely to remain in day care or preschool, without being asked to leave. They also had more friends during the time of the study.

A similar study by Castillo (2001) found the same basic result. They looked at children who were not specifically diagnosed with ADHD but showed some of the same symptoms. Once again, children who were taking stimulant medication were able to stay in the facility, while those who were not were often asked to leave.

Sample literature review without synthesis. From *Teaching APA Style to Beginners* (p. 5), by C. Reaves, 2004. Copyright 2004 by Celia Reaves. Reprinted with permission.

FIGURE 5.2

Giving stimulant medication such as Ritalin to very young children has some advantages. It makes them more compliant in school (Jones, 1998; Smith, 2000) and they are less likely to be asked to leave their daycare or preschool setting (Noloko, 1999). In addition, they make friends more easily (Smith, 2000; Weinburger, 1997).

On the other hand, some people point out serious drawbacks to this use of medication in very young children. Several researchers (Andrews, 1999; Castillo, 2001; Ngau & Mostomi, 1999) argue that these medications have never received FDA approval for such young patients because there is insufficient evidence that they are free of long-term complications. As Franklin (1998) puts it, "We are giving powerful drugs to children whose nervous systems are not yet developed. We don't know what can happen (p. 32)."

Sample literature review with synthesis. From *Teaching APA Style to Beginners* (p. 6), by C. Reaves, 2004. Copyright 2004 by Celia Reaves. Reprinted with permission.

Organizing a Literature Review

Depending on the course, instructor, and assignment, you may be asked to write a stand-alone literature review paper, as described previously. However, a more common type of literature review may be embedded in a larger paper, such as a research paper. This type of literature review might be for a research methods or experimental design class, for example. In this case, the literature review is actually part of the Introduction section, which is part of a larger manuscript.

In the following paragraphs, I present the instructions that I give to students when I assign a literature review as part of the Introduction section of a research paper. Depending on the assignment, you may be asked to follow a similar set of instructions. Generally, your literature review will be organized like this: (a) introduce the research question, demonstrating why it is important; (b) narrow the research question or studies to be discussed; (c) provide a brief outline or synopsis of the paper; (d) describe the studies in some detail; (e) compare and evaluate studies; and (f) discuss the implications of your studies (University of Washington, 2005). Although I have customized my instructions over the years, they originally came from an earlier edition of Bordens and Abbott (2004); I have also added to these additional information from the University of Wisconsin—Madison Writing Center (n.d.).

INTRODUCE THE TOPIC

Introduce the reader to the issue in the first paragraph by defining or identifying the general topic. Convince the reader that this is an important issue. Perhaps it affects a large number of people or is an essential component of daily life. Try to impress upon the reader the importance of the issue—in other words, why this topic is so important that it warrants research and the effort and resources necessary to conduct the research. Kendall, Silk, and Chu (2000) offered specific ideas for the opening paragraph, such as asking a rhetorical question, sharing an everyday experience, use of analogy, providing a striking statistical fact, or alluding to a historical event.

REVIEW THE LITERATURE

Review the available literature on the topic. If there are studies related specifically to your topic, review them here. If there are no specific studies, broaden your review of the literature to include related areas. Show that you have done your scholarly homework, and provide a context for your study. Point out overall trends in the published literature about this topic, using analysis, synthesis, and your idea notecards. Group research studies and other types of literature according to common denominators such as qualitative versus quantitative, objectives, methodology, and so forth. Discuss the general outcomes of each study and not the methodological details, unless those details are vital to your study.

IDENTIFY THE PROBLEM OR GAP IN KNOWLEDGE

Within this context, identify a problem or area in which the knowledge is incomplete. This becomes your statement of the problem to be addressed by your research. You have reviewed the literature, but there is a gap in the literature—an unresolved problem or issue. The goal of your study is to fill that gap. Explain why your study is important within the context of previous studies and the unanswered question.

STATE YOUR PURPOSE

Provide a clear statement of purpose for the current study. Be specific about the problem you are going to solve. Tell why this study is necessary to fill this gap in the research. In fact, it is often a good idea to signal this by including a sentence that begins "It is the purpose of this study to. . . ."

PREVIEW THE STUDY ("COMING ATTRACTIONS")

Next, give a brief overview of the methodology that will be used to address the knowledge gap. This should be just a snapshot of the participants, materials, and basic procedure used in the study.

NARROW YOUR FOCUS

What do you expect to happen? Conclude your Introduction section with the expected outcomes of the specific hypotheses to be tested. Develop your working hypotheses on the basis of your expectations and your review of the literature. Be as specific as possible. Well-written hypotheses actually provide guidance later as you determine the statistical approach you will take in analyzing your results. Good science requires that hypotheses be testable—your wording (e.g., an operational definition or definitions) is important here.

The introduction is just the first major part of a research paper (chapter 6 addresses all the major parts of the research paper, not just the Introduction section). A common analogy for a research paper is an hourglass, in which the introduction makes up most of the top half (see Figure 5.3). As you can see, both the hourglass and the Introduction section start very broad and then become more narrow and focused. (This, too, is the pattern of a research paper, in which, after narrowing, there will again be a broadening of approach.)

FIGURE 5.3

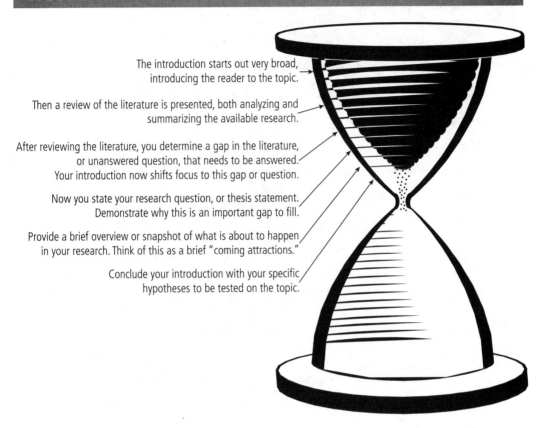

The introduction starts out very broad, introducing the reader to the topic.

Then a review of the literature is presented, both analyzing and summarizing the available research.

After reviewing the literature, you determine a gap in the literature, or unanswered question, that needs to be answered. Your introduction now shifts focus to this gap or question.

Now you state your research question, or thesis statement. Demonstrate why this is an important gap to fill.

Provide a brief overview or snapshot of what is about to happen in your research. Think of this as a brief "coming attractions."

Conclude your introduction with your specific hypotheses to be tested on the topic.

Hourglass model.

Sample Literature Review

In this section, I present an actual first draft of a literature review written by one of my students, Carol (I have used this work, and her name, with Carol's permission). When I say actual first draft, I should qualify that. Carol is a very good student and a good writer, and she agreed to share this work with me for this book. However, there were not that many errors in her first rough draft, which is, of course, a tribute to her work. Thus, you will see three variations of this introduction–literature review: an original rough draft (Figure 5.4); this rough draft marked, the way I would have marked it (Figure 5.5); and the final draft, as it actually appeared (Figure 5.6).

First look at Figure 5.4; then, look at Figure 5.5, with my editing marks. This is an interesting exercise on a number of dimensions. First,

FIGURE 5.4

Effects of Academic Stress on

the Nutritional Habits of College Students

In the competitive and stressful world of today's college student, who not only potentially carries a full academic load but more than likely works part to full-time, the hypothesis can be made that one of the first behaviors to be sacrificed is that of a healthy and nutritious diet. Our nutritional habits have a great deal to say about our ability to optimally perform in the world in which we live. Unfortunately, many find it easier to take the course of least resistance and allow healthy behaviors, such as healthy eating habits, to be modified by the level of stress being experienced. According to the Bureau of Labor Statistics (1999), missed work days due to occupational stress were more than four times the median absence for all occupational injuries and illnesses. Stress is an issue affecting everyone in all areas of endeavor, and subsequently, when everyday stressors lay their claim to already hectic schedules it is not unreasonable to expect repercussions in other areas of life.

Although previous research has been conducted regarding college student stress and a variety of behaviors that it affects, specifically the underlying causes of the inability to maintain a healthy diet during stressful times remains to be seen. What are the stress factors at play within the lives of college students that keep them from fulfilling this very basic and vital need? Verplanken and Faes (1999) examined this issue in light of what they termed "implementation intentions," which are concrete plans of action that specify when, where, and how actions should be taken to accomplish a specific goal. In the case of their study, this was directed toward the purposeful planning of a healthier diet by college students. Oaten and Cheng (2005) examined the idea that exertions of self-control will be followed by periods of diminished capacity, where, placing additional demands on students would potentially produce regulatory failures in other

Sample literature review, rough draft. From course literature review by Carol Pack, 2007. Copyright 2007 by Carol Pack. Printed with permission.

FIGURE 5.4 *(Continued)*

areas where lack of control had not previously been an issue. They hypothesized that many forms of self-control break down under stress, and that the stress of college could potentially cause an exertion of self-control that depletes an inner resource that allows regulation of other behaviors, such as healthy nutritional practices.

Understanding the attitudes and behaviors of students during stressful times would provide a starting point for the development of an approach to educating students about working through times of stress while continuing to maintain a healthy diet. This was the purpose of the study done by Soweid, El Kak, Major, Karam, and Roushana (2003) at the American University of Beirut. Students who attended a health awareness class were studied to see if they health information they received in the class would cause improved health attitudes and behaviors. The stress management abilities of the students attending this class showed significant improvement.

The goal of this study is to expand upon previous research regarding the attitudes and behaviors of college students under stress and how this stress affects their ability to practice healthy nutritional habits.

Participants will be drawn from a pool of Boise State University Psychology 101 students who are required to participate in four experiments for which they will receive class credit. They will be asked to complete a questionnaire regarding their perceived stress levels and their subsequent nutritional habits.

In this study, the expectation is to find that academic stress depletes a student's ability to regulate other voluntary behaviors, specifically those of healthy nutritional habits and practices. It is also anticipated that the diets of students will prove to be less healthy during the school year due to academic stress.

Sample literature review, rough draft. From course literature review by Carol Pack, 2007. Copyright 2007 by Carol Pack. Printed with permission.

FIGURE 5.5

Effects of Academic Stress on → *one line for title*

the Nutritional Habits of College Students

In the competitive and stressful world of today's college student, who not only potentially
carries a full academic load but more than likely works part to full-time, ~~the hypothesis can be~~ *I hypothesize* *awkward*
~~made~~ that one of the first behaviors to be sacrificed is that of a healthy *consuming* and nutritious diet. Our
nutritional habits ~~have a great deal~~ to ~~say about~~ *speak* our ability to optimally perform ~~in the world in~~
~~which we live.~~ Unfortunately, many find it easier to take the course of least resistance and allow
healthy behaviors, such as healthy eating habits, to be modified by the level of stress being
experienced. According to the Bureau of Labor Statistics (1999), missed work days due to
occupational stress were more than four times the median absence for all occupational injuries
and illnesses. Stress is an issue affecting everyone in all areas of endeavor, and ~~subsequently~~
when everyday stressors lay their claim to already hectic schedules it is not unreasonable to
expect repercussions in other areas of life.

Although previous research has been conducted regarding college student stress and a
variety of behaviors that it affects, specifically the underlying causes of the inability to maintain
a healthy diet during stressful times remains to be seen. What are the stress factors at play within
the lives of college students that keep them from fulfilling this very basic and vital need?
Verplanken and Faes (1999) examined this issue in light of what they termed "implementation
intentions," which are concrete plans of action that specify when, where, and how actions should
be taken to accomplish a specific goal. ~~In the case of their study~~ *(cap) study* this was directed toward the
purposeful planning of a healthier diet by college students. Oaten and Cheng (2005) examined
the idea that exertions of self-control will be followed by periods of diminished capacity, where,
placing additional demands on students would potentially produce regulatory failures in other

Sample literature review, with instructor's marks. From course literature review by Carol Pack, 2007. Copyright 2007 by Carol Pack. Adapted with permission.

FIGURE 5.5 (*Continued*)

These researchers

areas where lack of control had not previously been an issue. ~~They~~ hypothesized that many

forms of self-control break down under stress, and that the stress of college could potentially

cause ~~an~~ exertion of self-control that depletes an inner resource that allows regulation of other

behaviors, such as healthy nutritional practices.

Understanding the attitudes and behaviors of students during stressful times would

provide a starting point for the development of an approach to educating students about working

through times of stress while continuing to maintain a healthy diet. This was the purpose of the

conducted

study ~~done~~ by Soweid, El Kak, Major, Karam, and Roushana (2003) ~~at the American University~~ *not necessary*

~~of Beirut.~~ Students who attended a health awareness class were studied to see if ~~they~~ health

information ~~they~~ received in the class would cause improved health attitudes and behaviors. The

stress management abilities of the students attending this class showed significant improvement.

The goal of this study is to expand upon previous research regarding the attitudes and

behaviors of college students under stress and how this stress affects their ability to practice

healthy nutritional habits. *no need for a separate paragraph*

Participants will be drawn from a pool of Boise State University Psychology 101 students

this is incorrect !

who are required to participate in four experiments for which they will receive class credit. They

will be asked to complete a questionnaire regarding their perceived stress levels and ~~their~~

subsequent nutritional habits.

I expect

In this study, ~~the expectation is~~ to find that academic stress depletes a student's ability to

regulate other voluntary behaviors, specifically those of healthy nutritional habits and practices.

I

~~It is also~~ anticipated that the diets of students will ~~prove to~~ be less healthy during the school year

due to academic stress. *too strong*

Sample literature review, with instructor's marks. From course literature review by Carol Pack, 2007. Copyright 2007 by Carol Pack. Adapted with permission.

FIGURE 5.6

EFFECTS OF ACADEMIC STRESS   3

Effects of Academic Stress on the Nutritional Habits of College Students

In the competitive and stressful world of today's college student, who not only potentially carries a full academic load but more than likely works part-time or full-time, I hypothesize that one of the first behaviors to be sacrificed is the consumption of a healthy and nutritious diet. Our nutritional habits speak to our ability to optimally perform. Unfortunately, many find it easier to take the course of least resistance and allow healthy behaviors, such as healthy eating habits, to be modified by the level of stress being experienced. According to the Bureau of Labor Statistics (1999), missed work days due to occupational stress were more than 4 times the median absence for all occupational injuries and illnesses. Stress is an issue affecting everyone in all areas of endeavor and when everyday stressors lay their claim to already hectic schedules, it is not unreasonable to expect repercussions in other areas of life.

Although previous research has been conducted regarding college student stress and a variety of behaviors that it affects, specifically the underlying causes of the inability to maintain a healthy diet during stressful times remains to be seen. What are the stress factors at play within the lives of college students that keep them from fulfilling this very basic and vital need? Verplanken and Faes (1999) examined this issue in light of what they termed implementation intentions, which are concrete plans of action that specify when, where, and how actions should be taken to accomplish a specific goal. This was directed toward the purposeful planning of a healthier diet by college students. Oaten and Cheng (2005) examined the idea that exertions of self-control will be followed by periods of diminished capacity, where, placing additional demands on students would potentially produce regulatory failures in other areas where lack of control had not previously been an issue. These researchers hypothesized that many forms of self-control break down under stress, and that the stress of college could potentially cause

Sample literature review, final draft. From course literature review by Carol Pack, 2007. Copyright 2007 by Carol Pack. Adapted with permission.

FIGURE 5.6 (*Continued*)

EFFECTS OF ACADEMIC STRESS   4

exertion of self-control that depletes an inner resource that allows regulation of other behaviors,

such as healthy nutritional practices.

　　Understanding the attitudes and behaviors of students during stressful times would

provide a starting point for the development of an approach to educating students about working

through times of stress while continuing to maintain a healthy diet. This was the purpose of the

study conducted by Soweid, El Kak, Major, Karam, and Roushana (2003). Students who

attended a health awareness class were studied to see if health information received in the class

would cause improved health attitudes and behaviors. The stress management abilities of the

students attending this class showed significant improvement.

　　The goal of this study is to expand upon previous research regarding the attitudes and

behaviors of college students under stress and how this stress affects their ability to practice

healthy nutritional habits. Participants will be drawn from a pool of Boise State University

Psychology 101 students who are required to participate in some sort of research experience;

selecting the research participation option helps the student receive class credit. Students will be

asked to complete a questionnaire regarding their perceived stress levels and subsequent

nutritional habits. In this study, I expect to find that academic stress depletes a student's ability

to regulate other voluntary behaviors, specifically those of healthy nutritional habits and

practices. I anticipate that the diets of students will be less healthy during the school year due to

academic stress.

Sample literature review, final draft. From course literature review by
Carol Pack, 2007. Copyright 2007 by Carol Pack. Adapted with permission.

editing is often subjective; I made suggestions on Carol's paper that I thought would improve it. These weren't errors, per se, but stylistic suggestions. Second, another faculty member (or you, for that matter) might mark this paper quite differently than I did. I probably let some things go that others would not. For instance, the last part of the introduction uses the future tense. This was okay with me because during the class, students wrote their Introduction sections before they had conducted their study. Third, there were no running heads included with the first draft, which I was okay with when the assignment was first handed in. Now look at the finished product in Figure 5.6.

If you closely compare the edited draft with the final draft, you will note that Carol did not make all the corrections I suggested, which is fine. She also corrected some items I did not point out. This constant revising and editing is all part of the process of scientific writing in psychology.

How did Carol do with respect to the criteria from Galvan (2006) I presented earlier? In looking at the last draft of Carol's introduction, the first paragraph is particularly strong. She tells us why her topic is important ("Our nutritional habits speak to our ability to optimally perform"), and she also differentiates between research findings and other opinions by citing research from the Bureau of Labor Statistics. She ends her first paragraph by identifying the broad problem area.

In the second paragraph, Carol does a good job of indicating why certain studies are important, but I would have liked a more comprehensive review of the available studies. The studies she chose to review are both timely and applicable, but it seems that there must be much more available on this topic, and even a passing reference to that information with a few more references would be preferable. In looking at Carol's work, however, remember that her assignment was not just a literature review, but the Introduction section to her paper for a research methods class. Thus, after the literature review she continues to outline the gap in the literature and preview the study to be discussed in the remainder of the manuscript. As always, be sure to heed the instructor's criteria for an assignment, even if those criteria vary from American Psychological Association style or the suggestions in this book. In the next chapter, the story we started with the literature review will be continued throughout a research paper.

Telling an Original Story Through a Research Paper 6

It is best to do things systematically, since we are only human, and disorder is our worst enemy.

—*Hesiod*, Works and Days

Many of the types of scientific writing that you will be asked to complete in your psychology classes will be variations on the theme of this chapter—writing the research paper—and yes, that process is quite organized and systematic. A lab report is often a miniature version of a research paper, and a literature review is but one component of a research paper's Introduction section. Because of the importance of the research paper format and the necessity of using American Psychological Association (APA) format and style, this chapter presents in detail real examples of research paper sections, culminating in a complete paper.

To make the paper preparation process more real for you, just as I presented in chapter 5 Carol's original draft of an Introduction section–literature review, my edited copy, and her final draft, here I present the work of another student, Naiara (with her permission). I present sections of her research paper in the same way as I would assign them in my research methods class—the Introduction section first; then the Method, Results, and Discussion sections; followed by a combined assignment including the title page, abstract, references, and tables (which I call TPART—these details are covered in chapter 7); and then the completed final draft (also presented in chapter 7). To actively demonstrate this process for you, I present Naiara's original draft of each assignment, my marked-up copy of each assignment, and at the end of the chapter her completed paper. Note that I have purposely kept these examples real—that is, this is a real paper, and these are my real marks. I have not presented a perfect paper to you, but a very good paper completed by a very good student. My editing marks do not identify all the possible errors in the draft, and your instructor will certainly find mistakes that I did not. The final draft that you see is not absolutely perfect, but for the assignment I gave and in the time frame in which it was completed, I consider it outstanding work. I appreciate both Naiara and Carol for generously sharing their work for your benefit.

Set the Tone: Introduction and Sample

In the previous chapter, I presented a sample Introduction section, including the literature review; however, the Introduction section is important enough that some points bear repeating. When you start to write your introduction, you will begin to realize how different scientific writing is from other types of writing. Scientific writing is not as personal as writing a personal narrative, short story, or poem; rather, it is detached and objective. Even though you may be describing your personal research, you should not be personal in your writing. One of the best ways to understand this "tone" of writing is by reading examples from psychological journals. Note that the better journal articles are easier to read; if you cannot understand the gist of an article after reading it, then I would argue that the article wasn't well written. Good science involves communication of new knowledge, and poorly written research papers and articles are poor because they fail to communicate clearly.

As depicted in chapter 5, the shape of a manuscript resembles that of an hourglass (a common analogy; see Bem, 2004). Your introduction starts broadly and becomes more and more narrow until you finish with specific hypotheses and predictions about the research to be presented. How many references should be cited in your Introduction section? There is no definitive answer unless your instructor indicates this to you as part of the assignment. The literature review of a research paper is not meant to be exhaustive. The goal instead is to report on the classic, seminal work in the field and provide a current update on the present knowledge (Calderon & Austin, 2006). Using examples to help illustrate important or complicated material is an excellent way to communicate to the reader and demonstrate your thorough understanding of the concepts being presented (Bem, 2004).

A sample first draft of Naiara's Introduction section appears in Figure 6.1. My edited copy appears in Figure 6.2. (As noted earlier, the complete, final draft copy appears at the end of chapter 7.) Note that Naiara correctly numbered the first page of the Introduction section as page 3. She knew that sections she would later complete would appear before the Introduction section—the title page on page 1 and the abstract on page 2. Also note that the word *Introduction* does not appear at the top of the page—instead, APA format dictates that the title from page 1 be repeated at the beginning of the Introduction section.

Total Transparency: Method Section and Sample

The Method section tells the reader exactly how the study was conducted. You describe your participants, materials, and procedure in three separate subsections of the Method section. Although the Method section may appear to be dry reading, it is important! The Method section provides a blueprint for other researchers, especially if they want to replicate (repeat) your study. In psychology and other sciences, we don't keep secrets. We tell the world exactly how we conducted our study, down to the nitty-gritty details. Your study should be an open book, and your Method section should provide enough detail that if another researcher wanted to replicate your study, he or she would be able to do so. This open, objective feature is an important component of science— the transparency of one's method.

PARTICIPANTS

Tell the reader who participated in your study. In this section, you need to report (a) who took part in the study, (b) how many participants there were, (c) how the participants were selected, and (d) any pertinent demographic variables. Typically, demographic variables include sex (gender), age, and race or ethnicity. (Note: If you are reporting the mean [average] age, remember that you must also reports its corresponding standard deviation. In APA format, every mean must be accompanied by a standard deviation.) Report here any demographic variables that are related to the hypotheses you are testing. For example, if you were conducting a study on political attitudes about some aspect of governmental functioning, it might be an important demographic to report the breakdown of Republican, Democrat, and Independent participants. Also report how you selected participants or whether participants self-selected or volunteered to complete

FIGURE 6.1

VALUE OF PHYSICAL INTERACTION   3

The Value of Physical Interaction in a Romantic Relationship

That first smile, the first look of compassion and care, the first soft touch after a compliment given, the first long gaze, every first interaction with someone new that brings about a feeling of joy and excitement—why be without? Humans yearn for a feeling of intimacy and connection with one another because it is in our nature. People need someone to lift them when they are down, wipe their tears when they are sad, embrace them in times of happiness and encourage them in times of doubt. Every person who has had a romantic partner to share this with knows the true significance of interaction. Every minute spent with this person is another minute the two grow close and learn from each other. Being able to look into someone's eyes when confessions of love are being made, concern is being expressed, or truth is being sought is invaluable. Nothing can replace that someone being right there in front of you. These experiences are why the quantity and quality of physical interaction are such vital parts of maintaining a romantic relationship. Previous researchers may have recognized and stressed the importance of interaction in general, however, the question being asked here is which aspect of interaction is the most important, the quality or quantity?

Every couple wants a successful relationship that is also satisfying. Partners who are satisfied with their interactions tend to be satisfied with their overall relationships (Emmers-Sommer, 2004). In order to reach this satisfaction, one would assume that interactions between partners needed to be both frequent and fulfilling. As a response to ongoing interaction between partners, love attitudes are formed which are characteristics of each person shaped by personality type, past and existing relationship interactions (Meeks, Hendrick & Hendrick, 1998). These love attitudes are also factors in determining relationship satisfaction. Having recurrent interactions with a partner would allow for an abundance of occasions to learn about the person and over

Introduction section of sample research paper, rough draft. From course research paper by Naiara Arozamena, 2007. Copyright 2007 by Naiara Arozamena. Adapted with permission.

FIGURE 6.1 *(Continued)*

VALUE OF PHYSICAL INTERACTION   4

time decide personal relationship satisfaction. However, one might feel that the quality of the interaction, even though possibly brief, eventually determines this same romantic relationship satisfaction. Either way, people interact when they are doing things together, and doing things together usually results in positive relational experiences (Emmers-Sommer, 2004).

So which aspect of interaction in a relationship is more important, the amount of interaction, or the quality of it? Arguments for both sides have been made in one way, shape or form. For example, Emmers-Sommer (2004) found that contact frequency is not necessarily mandatory for a close relationship, but that frequency of in-person contact is significant in relational satisfaction. However, self-disclosure defined as face-to-face communication of personal information by calls for cooperative interaction and is often reciprocal, therefore related to the development of close personal ties (Arliss, 1991). Two partners might not be able to fully self-disclose without being in proximity of one another, with that ever so important eye-contact and physical presence. This difference of opinion brings about a conflict regarding the true importance of each of these aspects of interaction. Both have been suggested to be more pertinent than the other, but neither argument has had much solid data collected to show this.

The goal of this study is to inspect and evaluate the differences and importance of the quality and quantity of physical interaction in a heterosexual romantic relationship. The method of research for this study will be the distribution of a survey to undergraduate Psychology 101 students at Boise State University. Gender and age data will be collected, as well as the duration of participants' romantic relationships.

Emerging from the data examined and studied so far are the following proposed hypotheses:

H1 The increase in the quality of interaction positively influences relationship intimacy.

Introduction section of sample research paper, rough draft. From course research paper by Naiara Arozamena, 2007. Copyright 2007 by Naiara Arozamena. Adapted with permission.

FIGURE 6.1 (*Continued*)

VALUE OF PHYSICAL INTERACTION   5

It is expected that the participants' disclosure on the quality of their relationship interaction has had a positive effect on their romantic relationship.

    H2 Men's perception of physical interaction may frequently be more sexual, whereas women's perception may be more emotional.

Data will be collected in attempt to show that the definitions of physical interaction usually differ between opposite sexes, but contain similarities between same sexes.

    H3 The ability to self-disclose positively increases the quality of a relationship.

The importance and results of using self-disclosure in a romantic relationship will be examined and hopefully support this hypothesis. Having the ability to open up to someone seems to be a vital and necessary component in maintaining a healthy and productive relationship.

    H4 The quality of long-distance relationships can be greater than that of a proximal one, even though the frequency of interaction is lessened.

The status of the proximity of the participants' relationships will be asked about as well as interaction quality, in attempt to refute that proximity is essential for a satisfactory relationship.

Introduction section of sample research paper, rough draft. From course research paper by Naiara Arozamena, 2007. Copyright 2007 by Naiara Arozamena. Adapted with permission.

your study. The general terms *subjects* and *participants* are now in common usage.

MATERIALS (OR APPARATUS)

Describe all the materials used to conduct the study. Essentially, this is a listing of the equipment needed to conduct the study. Did you use a computer to present stimulus items on the screen? Did you videotape participants and later analyze their behavior? Did you develop a survey and then administer it to participants? Were you involved in any pilot testing before working with actual participants? Describe the materials

FIGURE 6.2

VALUE OF PHYSICAL INTERACTION   3

The Value of Physical Interaction in a Romantic Relationship

That first smile, the first look of compassion and care, the first soft touch after a

compliment given, the first long gaze, every first interaction with someone new that brings about

a feeling of joy and excitement. Why be without? Humans yearn for a feeling of intimacy and

connection with one another because it is in our nature. People need someone to lift them when

they are down, wipe their tears when they are sad, embrace them in times of happiness and

encourage them in times of doubt. Every person who has had a romantic partner to share this

— too strong; These are overstatements

with knows the true significance of interaction. Every minute spent with this person is another

minute the two grow close and learn from each other. Being able to look into someone's eyes

when confessions of love are being made, concern is being expressed, or truth is being sought is

invaluable. Nothing can replace that someone being right there in front of you. These

specific examples?

experiences are why the quantity and quality of physical interaction are such vital parts of

avoid passive voice

maintaining a romantic relationship. Previous researchers may have recognized and stressed the

importance of interaction in general; however, the question being asked here is which aspect of

interaction is the most important, the quality or quantity?

Every couple wants a successful relationship that is also satisfying. Partners who are

satisfied with their interactions tend to be satisfied with their overall relationships (Emmers-

might

Sommer, 2004). In order to reach this satisfaction, one would assume that interactions between

partners needed to be both frequent and fulfilling. As a response to ongoing interaction between

awkward—what do you mean?

partners, love attitudes are formed which are characteristics of each person shaped by personality

type, past and existing relationship interactions (Meeks, Hendrick & Hendrick, 1998). These love

attitudes are also factors in determining relationship satisfaction. Having recurrent interactions

with a partner would allow for an abundance of occasions to learn about the person and over

Introduction section of sample research paper with instructor's editing marks. From course research paper by Naiara Arozamena, 2007. Copyright 2007 by Naiara Arozamena. Adapted with permission.

FIGURE 6.2 (Continued)

VALUE OF PHYSICAL INTERACTION   4

time decide personal relationship satisfaction. However, one might feel that the quality of the

interaction, even though possibly brief, eventually determines this same romantic relationship

satisfaction. Either way, people interact when they are doing (things) together, and doing (things)   *Too vague — avoid*

together usually results in positive relational experiences (Emmers-Sommer, 2004).

So which aspect of interaction in a relationship is more important, the amount of

interaction, or the quality of it? Arguments for both sides ~~have been made in one way, shape or~~   *are available*) *Avoid passive voice.*

~~form.~~ For example, Emmers-Sommer (2004) found that contact frequency is not necessarily

mandatory for a close relationship, but that frequency of in-person contact is significant in

relational satisfaction. However, self-disclosure defined as face-to-face communication of

personal information by calls for cooperative interaction and is often reciprocal, therefore related

to the development of close personal ties (Arliss, 1991). Two partners might not be able to fully

self-disclose without being in proximity of one another, with that ever so important eye-contact

and physical presence. This difference of opinion brings about a conflict regarding the ~~true~~   *among researchers*

importance of each of these aspects of interaction. ~~Both have been suggested to be more~~

~~pertinent than the other, but neither argument has had much solid data collected to show this.~~

The goal of this study is to inspect and evaluate the differences and importance of the

quality and quantity of physical interaction in a heterosexual romantic relationship. The method

of research for this study ~~will be~~ *is* the distribution of a survey to undergraduate *general* Psychology ~~101~~

students at Boise State University. Gender and age data ~~will be~~ *are* collected, as well as the duration

of participants' romantic relationships.

Emerging from the data examined and studied so far are the following proposed

hypotheses:

Write these in completion sentences — you can use seriation (a) (b) (c) (d)

~~H1~~ (a) The increase in the quality of interaction positively influences relationship intimacy.

Introduction section of sample research paper with instructor's editing
marks. From course research paper by Naiara Arozamena, 2007.
Copyright 2007 by Naiara Arozamena. Adapted with permission.

FIGURE 6.2 (*Continued*)

VALUE OF PHYSICAL INTERACTION   5

It is expected that the participants' disclosure on the quality of their relationship interaction ~~has~~
~~had a~~ positive *ly* effect ~~on their~~ *a* romantic relationship.

(*b*) ~~H2~~ Men's perception of physical interaction may frequently be more sexual, whereas
women's perception may be more emotional.

I expect
~~Data will be collected in attempt to show~~ that the definitions of physical interaction usually differ
between opposite sexes, but contain similarities between same sexes. *as well*

(*c*) ~~H3~~ The ability to self-disclose positively increases the quality of a relationship.

is
The importance and results of using self-disclosure in a romantic relationship ~~will be~~ examined
~~and hopefully support this hypothesis.~~ Having the ability to open up to someone ~~seems~~ *appears* to be a
vital and necessary component in maintaining a healthy and productive relationship.

(*d*) ~~H4~~ The quality of long-distance relationships can be greater than that of a proximal one,
even though the frequency of interaction is lessened.

is ascertained
The status of the proximity of the participants' relationships ~~will be asked about~~ as well as
interaction quality, in attempt to refute that proximity is essential for a satisfactory relationship.

Method section should continue
Here in the final paper —
just regular double-spacing.

Introduction section of sample research paper with instructor's editing
marks. From course research paper by Naiara Arozamena, 2007.
Copyright 2007 by Naiara Arozamena. Adapted with permission.

used to such a degree that someone else would be able to recreate them, or find your sources and obtain them. If you developed original survey questions, include them in a table or appendix. If you used a specialized computer program, be sure to give the details so that someone else would be able to obtain and use a similar program. The term *apparatus* refers to the specialized equipment that a study may have required. Not every Method section will have an Apparatus section.

PROCEDURE

This section of your Method section describes how the study was completed from the first step to the last step. Provide enough information about the procedure followed so that another researcher could replicate the study. This might include the instructions given to participants if the instructions are an important part of the independent variable manipulation in your study. Describe how participants were assigned to groups or subgroups, addressing issues such as randomization or counterbalancing (as appropriate). If you developed a new technique, describe it in enough detail that others could replicate it. Be sure to include any debriefing accounts if that is part of your research study.

In my research methods course, Naiara developed a small set of survey questions that were added to a larger set from the entire class. Given that this is a survey study, the details are fairly straightforward. I present her first rough draft of the Method section in Figure 6.3 and my marked-up version in Figure 6.4.

What Happened, but Not Why: Results Section and Sample

The major purpose of the Results section is to report the findings of your research. If you are going to include a table or figure, it is usually referred to somewhere in the Results section. Every hypothesis mentioned at the end of your Introduction section must be specifically addressed in your Results section, regardless of whether the hypothesis was supported or not. Follow APA format for the reporting of descriptive and inferential statistics. For instance, in descriptive statistics, every time you report a mean you need to report its corresponding standard deviation, thus providing a measure of central tendency and a measure of variability, respectively. When using inferential statistics, you need to italicize the symbol representing the statistic (e.g., r, t, or F) and include a p value statement toward the end of your sentence (be sure to check with your

FIGURE 6.3

VALUE OF PHYSICAL INTERACTION   1

Method

Participants

    For this study, 60 participants from Boise State University were used to help gather the

necessary information. The Psychology 101 students ranging from ages 18 through 30 (M =

20.87, SD = 3.14) were recruited using a program called Experimetrix. The participants consisted

of 28 males and 30 females (two participants did not specify their gender) of all different

relationship statuses (single, divorced, married, engaged and boyfriend/girlfriend). For those

participants in an intimate relationship, the duration of that relationship was asked for in months,

(M = 14.15, SD = 18.94). The participants were selected by their volunteering to participate and

were rewarded with points for their Psychology 101 course.

Materials

    Survey questions were developed entirely by the author, driven by the formed

hypotheses. The materials were pilot tested. To clearly read and understand the information

being studied and the survey questions asked, please refer to Table 1.

Procedure

    The study was conducted in a large lecture room with all of the participants present, as

well as the author. The questions in Table 1 were a part of a larger survey being administered.

The room was kept silent while the participants were given 60 minutes to individually complete

the 190-question survey. The survey was anonymous. Following completion of the survey,

participants were debriefed and thanked.

Method section of sample research paper, rough draft. From course
research paper by Naiara Arozamena, 2007. Copyright 2007 by
Naiara Arozamena. Adapted with permission.

FIGURE 6.4

VALUE OF PHYSICAL INTERACTION   1

Method

Participants

For this study, 60 participants from Boise State University were used to help gather the

necessary information. The Psychology 101 ~~students~~ students ranging from ~~ages~~ 18 through 30 ($M =$

20.87, $SD = 3.14$) were recruited using a program called Experimetrix. The participants consisted

of 28 males and 30 females (two participants did not specify their gender) of all different

relationship statuses (single, divorced, married, engaged, and boyfriend/girlfriend). For those

participants in an intimate relationship, the duration of that relationship was asked ~~for~~ about in months

($M = 14.15$, $SD = 18.94$). The participants were selected by their volunteering to participate and

were rewarded with points for their Psychology 101 course.

Materials

~~Survey questions were~~ I developed entirely by the author, driven by the formed the survey questions to attempt to address

my hypotheses. The materials were pilot tested. To ~~clearly read and understand the information~~ see

~~being studied and~~ the survey questions asked, please refer to Table 1.

Procedure

The study was conducted in a large lecture room with all of the participants present ~~as~~

~~well as the author.~~ The questions in Table 1 were a part of a larger survey being administered.

The room was kept silent while the participants were given 60 ~~minutes~~ to individually complete

the 190 question survey. The survey ~~was~~ responses were anonymous. Following completion of the survey,

participants were debriefed and thanked.

Method section of sample research paper with instructor's editing marks.
From course research paper by Naiara Arozamena, 2007. Copyright 2007
by Naiara Arozamena. Adapted with permission.

instructor to see whether he or she wants a measure of effect size included with your statistical results). Start your Results section with the outcome that is most important to your research (Salovey, 2000); I tell my students to start with the "big bang" of the findings—that is, report the most important finding first.

Bem (2004) suggested the following sequence for the presentation of information in the Results section:

1. Verify that your study was successful in setting up the conditions needed to adequately test your hypothesis (i.e., that nothing major went wrong in the conduct of the study).
2. Describe your overall approach to data analysis, including the methodology used to obtain your dependent variable measurements.
3. Provide a brief reminder of the main conceptual question or hypothesis, and a reminder about the basic tests performed and behaviors measured. Why? Because sometimes readers will read parts of a research paper (or journal article) out of order. The reminders are a courtesy to the readers and save them the extra work of looking for the context to interpret the section they are reading.
4. Answer your hypotheses as clearly and unequivocally as you can, using words, then your statistical evidence in numbers, in APA format.
5. After addressing the major hypotheses of the study, address other findings or surprises that emerged. Use the same format—describe what happened clearly, in words, then numbers.
6. You may want to organize your Results section into logical subsections if that will help the reader follow the story. Be sure to use the proper APA-style headings as signposts, just as you did with the Participants, Materials, and Procedure subsections of the Method section.
7. As you move from paragraph to paragraph in the Results section, try to provide smooth transitions between paragraphs, emphasizing the logical flow of your hypothesis testing and the outcomes of your research.

Plonsky (2006) offered additional advice on what *not* to do in a Results section: (a) do not discuss the implications of the results in the Results section; that is saved for the Discussion section; (b) do not discuss the alpha level or the null hypothesis because most readers in the scientific community will already understand these assumptions; (c) do not organize subsections of your Results section by type of analysis (all the *t* tests in one paragraph, all the correlations in the next); instead, organize subsections by variable to be studied or hypothesis to be tested;

(d) do not present the raw data collected, unless that is part of your instructor's assignment; and (e) do not use the word *proved* because in science we never prove anything, we only disprove competing theories and hypotheses until one logical explanation is left standing—we hope, our working hypothesis.

In the assignment for Naiara's research paper, I require that students report their survey data in two subsections—a section on descriptive statistics and another on question-by-question analyses. So if you are wondering why Naiara's descriptive statistics section is so short, well, she was following the instructions of her instructor! Figure 6.5 presents her rough draft; Figure 6.6 presents my marked-up copy.

Explain and Question Again: Discussion Section and Sample

In the Discussion section, you finally get the chance to interpret all the results that were presented in the Results section. Here is where you have the opportunity to finish telling the story that you began in the Introduction section. What happened? What worked, and what did not work? What will the reader be able to conclude from your study? The Discussion section starts out very specific—what happened in this study—and gets broader until you finish with generalizations and conclusions. Essentially, the Discussion section is the bottom of the hourglass—it starts out narrow, with answers to your specific hypotheses, and ends broad, with the implications of your study for future researchers.

As with the Introduction section, I provide students with the six items I look for in a Discussion section. Not every item will be its own paragraph, and some items may require more than one paragraph. I provide a template below. Remember, after you've read more psychology journal articles and written more psychology research papers, you'll feel comfortable moving away from the template and into your own style that fits within APA format. Not every Discussion section I have ever written has these six points precisely represented, but this template is a good starting point.

Start your Discussion with the most important finding of the study—what I call the "big bang" of your study. What happened? Did you find anything that was unexpected, unusual, fascinating, interesting, unique, or counterintuitive? The first paragraph of your Discussion section should have the "take-home" message for the reader—if the reader is to remember only one piece of information from this study, what is it? The major premise of your study should be described here—whether something turned out the way you expected or didn't turn out the way you expected.

FIGURE 6.5

VALUE OF PHYSICAL INTERACTION   3

Results

Descriptive Statistics

Please refer to Table 1 for all the means and standard deviations of the survey questions.

Question-by-Question Analyses

The first hypothesis is that the increase in the quality of interaction positively influences relationship intimacy. When examining the effects of gender using a t test with the survey item "I am currently in an intimate relationship" using an agreement scale from 1 = strongly disagree to 5 = strongly agree, there is a significant difference between males ($M = 2.65$, $SD = 1.38$) and females ($M = 3.66$, $SD = 1.58$) on intimate relationship status, $t(54) = -2.530$, $p < .05$. When examining the item "I physically interact with my partner" using a frequency scale from 0 = never to 3 = always, there is a significant difference between males ($M = 1.29$, $SD = 1.08$) and females ($M = 2.17$, $SD = .88$) on frequency of interaction scores, $t(45) = -3.049$, $p < .05$. A t test was also used to examine the relationship between agreement scale item "Sharing personal thoughts, feelings and experiences with my partner increases the quality of our relationship" and agreement scale 1 = yes and 0 = no item "Over the duration of my relationship, our physical interaction has increased. A significant difference was found between the participants who answered "yes" ($M = 4.43$, $SD = .56$) and those who answered "no" ($M = 3.94$, $SD = .65$) on self-disclosure scores, $t(45) = 2.693$, $p < .05$.

Of the 54 participants who responded by agreement scale for the item "The more positive interaction I have with my partner, the more intimate our relationship becomes," 33 answered agree and 13 answered strongly agree (totaling 85.2%), while only 8 said anything less (14.8%). In support of Hypothesis 1, there is a significant correlation between the item "The more positive

Results section of sample research paper, rough draft. From course research paper by Naiara Arozamena, 2007. Copyright 2007 by Naiara Arozamena. Adapted with permission.

FIGURE 6.5 (*Continued*)

VALUE OF PHYSICAL INTERACTION   4

interaction, the more intimate," and item "Sharing personal thoughts...increases relationship

quality," $r(50) = .465, p < .01$.

The second hypothesis suggests that the ability to self-disclose positively increases the

quality of a relationship. This prediction was sustained by the significant correlation between

agreement scale item "I feel that I can self-disclose and open up to my partner," and the item

"Sharing . . . with my partner increases relationship quality," $r(51) = .733, p < .01$. This

hypothesis was also supported by the item "I feel I can self-disclose," which significantly

correlates with frequency scale-based item "I physically interact with my partner," $r(45) = .337$,

$p < .05$.

Results section of sample research paper, rough draft. From course research paper by Naiara Arozamena, 2007. Copyright 2007 by Naiara Arozamena. Adapted with permission.

Briefly restate the hypotheses from the end of your Introduction section and discuss whether they were supported on the basis of the study's outcomes. Be specific (e.g., "Significant gender differences were found for the questions regarding X, X, and X. In all cases, men were more favorable toward these questions than women. This means that. . . ."). Thus, all hypotheses, whether supported or not, are addressed somewhere in the Discussion section. Place your study in the context of the studies that have come before yours. This means revisiting some of the literature you cited in the Introduction section. Re-cite some of that literature here.

Did you fill that knowledge gap or hole that you identified early on? Whereas you may have answered one question, perhaps your study raised three new ones (this is typical in psychological research—it's called job security!). If your study contradicts previous research, then you need to speculate about why that happened—for example, perhaps it was a different subject population or the methodologies were dramatically different. The reader knows when you are in this section of the Discussion because citations (with author names and publication years) appear again.

FIGURE 6.6

VALUE OF PHYSICAL INTERACTION   3

Results

Descriptive Statistics

Please refer to Table 1 for all the means and standard deviations of the survey questions.

Question-by-Question Analyses

The first hypothesis is that the increase in the quality of interaction positively influences

relationship intimacy. When examining the effects of gender using a *t* test with the survey item

"I am currently in an intimate relationship" using an agreement scale from 1 = strongly disagree   *italics*

to 5 = strongly agree, there is a significant difference between males ($M = 2.65$, $SD = 1.38$) and   *italics*

females ($M = 3.66$, $SD = 1.58$) on intimate relationship status, $t(54) = -2.539$, $p < .05$. When   *report exact p value*

examining the item "I physically interact with my partner" using a frequency scale from 0 =

never to 3 = always, there is a significant difference between males ($M = 1.29$, $SD = 1.08$) and   *italics*

females ($M = 2.17$, $SD = .88$) on frequency of interaction scores, $t(45) = -3.049$, $p < .05$. A *t* test   *5*

was also used to examine the relationship between agreement scale item "Sharing personal

thoughts, feelings and experiences with my partner increases the quality of our relationship" and

agreement scale 1 = yes and 0 = no item "Over the duration of my relationship, our physical   *italics*

interaction has increased. A significant difference was found between the participants who

answered "yes" ($M = 4.43$, $SD = .56$) and those who answered "no" ($M = 3.94$, $SD = .65$) on self-

disclosure scores, $t(45) = 2.69$, $p < .05$.

Of the 54 participants who responded by agreement scale for the item "The more positive

interaction I have with my partner, the more intimate our relationship becomes," 33 answered

agree and 13 answered strongly agree (totaling 85.2%), while only 8 said anything less (14.8%).   *whereas*

In support of Hypothesis 1, there is a significant correlation between the item "The more positive   *answers to*

Results section of sample research paper with instructor's editing marks.
From course research paper by Naiara Arozamena, 2007. Copyright 2007
by Naiara Arozamena. Adapted with permission.

FIGURE 6.6 (Continued)

VALUE OF PHYSICAL INTERACTION   4

interaction, the more intimate," and item "Sharing personal thoughts...increases relationship

quality," $r(50) = .46$, $p < .01$. — *report exact p value*

The second hypothesis suggests that the ability to self-disclose positively increases the

quality of a relationship. This prediction was sustained by the significant correlation between

the agreement scale item "I feel that I can self-disclose and open up to my partner," and the item

"Sharing . . . with my partner increases relationship quality," $r(51) = .73$, $p < .01$. This

hypothesis was also supported by the item "I feel I can self-disclose," which significantly

correlated with frequency scale-based item "I physically interact with my partner," $r(45) = .33$,

$p < .05$.

Discussion section would follow here, with regular double-spacing.

Results section of sample research paper with instructor's editing marks.
From course research paper by Naiara Arozamena, 2007. Copyright 2007
by Naiara Arozamena. Adapted with permission.

Now generalize a bit about the results of your study. Look beyond, to a broader context than just those tested. Here you get to speculate on the greater impact of your research, but be sure to label speculation as such. What do the results of your study mean? In other words, could the results of your study be useful in setting policies about human behavior? How might they be interpreted in a broader context beyond the sample you studied?

Present the limitations of your study, but don't beat up on yourself too much—no study has ever been conducted perfectly. In general, write the Discussion section as if everything was measured perfectly. In this section of the Discussion, you present what went wrong—what do you wish you had done differently? Did you have enough participants to adequately test your hypotheses? What should be the next study?

Make some suggestions as to the direction of future research in this field. What do you suggest be done next?

Conclude your Discussion section with a brief paragraph that (a) restates your take-home message (the big bang), (b) reiterates the importance of your study in filling an existing knowledge gap in the literature, and (c) emphasizes the general importance of your topic. This helps justify to the reader the worthiness of your work, and it provides a nice broad completion to the bottom of the hourglass. As Bem (2004) put it, "End with a bang, not a whimper" (p. 203).

Naiara's first draft of her Discussion section is included in Figure 6.7; my editorial marks are in Figure 6.8.

The four sections presented in this chapter—Introduction, Method, Results, and Discussion—constitute the bulk of the research article. However, there are still several important details to attend to before your research paper is complete. How to complete those final details with style is the topic of the next chapter.

FIGURE 6.7

VALUE OF PHYSICAL INTERACTION   1

Discussion

Both the quality and quantity of physical interaction were previously stated to be important to a romantic relationship. However, in this study the more a couple self-disclosed and increased the quality of interaction in their intimate relationship, the higher the value, satisfaction, and intimacy of the relationship as a whole. Noticeably more support was found for the significance of quality in a relationship than the quantity. The ability to be able to open up, self-disclose, and be vulnerable with a partner has been shown to increase interaction in general. In other words, being able to let one's guard down and truly make the time with one's partner as rich and fulfilling as it can be may in many cases make the desire and need for interaction greater and greater.

Both of the predicted hypotheses stated in this research were supported by the data. In support of the first hypothesis, the increase in the quality of interaction positively influences relationship intimacy, significant gender differences were found for survey questions regarding intimate relationship status and frequency of interaction. In both cases, females were more likely to think of themselves as being in an intimate relationship, as well as feeling that they have more frequent interaction with their partner than the males do. This means that the personal definitions of "intimate relationship" and "interaction" are different for men and women. Also in support of this hypothesis, a significant correlation was found when examining the survey item "Sharing personal thoughts, feelings and experiences with my partner increases the quality of our relationship" and comparing it with the results from item "The more positive interaction I have with my partner, the more intimate our relationship becomes." In this case, the significant positive correlation of these two items solidifies that sharing personal thoughts, feelings and experiences would not only enhance the quality of the relationship, but would also positively

Discussion section of sample research paper, rough draft. From course research paper by Naiara Arozamena, 2007. Copyright 2007 by Naiara Arozamena. Adapted with permission.

FIGURE 6.7 (*Continued*)

VALUE OF PHYSICAL INTERACTION   2

affect relationship intimacy. This means that, as predicted, the increase of interaction quality in a relationship tends to lead to an increase in overall interaction and intimacy.

In support of the second hypothesis, the ability to self-disclose positively increases the quality of a relationship, the item "I feel that I can self-disclose and open up to my partner" was significantly correlated with "Sharing…with my partner increases relationship quality." This positive correlation indicates that the ability and comfort of a partner to self-disclose will lead to a higher quality relationship. This second hypothesis may also be supported by some of the results which supported the first hypothesis.

The purpose of Meeks, Hendrick, and Hendrick's (1998) study "was to develop a more comprehensive perspective on the associations among several conceptually related constructs and relationship satisfaction" (p. 762). They found that constructs such as conflict tactics, self-disclosure, and perspective taking were correlated with satisfaction in romantic relationships. Similarly, the current research was used to and did find that relationship interaction quality (which was found to be increased by self-disclosure) is more significant to a romantic relationship than interaction quantity. This finding was also supported by Emmers-Sommer (2004), "contact frequency is not necessarily mandatory for a close relationship" (p. 408). Also, the current study proposes that self-disclosure is in itself, a very personal form of interaction between partners. Previous research has agreed by stating, "Self-disclosing is termed an interactional event because it is assumed that sharing such information, in a dyadic situation, requires the participation of two willing partners and is likely to affect both of them and the relationship between them (Arliss, 1991). The results of this study may have only filled a small gap that was left by previous studies; however, they also placed a larger emphasis on the importance of quality interaction in a romantic relationship.

Discussion section of sample research paper, rough draft. From course research paper by Naiara Arozamena, 2007. Copyright 2007 by Naiara Arozamena. Adapted with permission.

FIGURE 6.7 (*Continued*)

VALUE OF PHYSICAL INTERACTION   3

    Based on the results of this study, one can speculate that positive, quality time two people spend together in a romantic relationship is not only more important that the amount of time they spend, it is also essential for growth, happiness, and overall relationship satisfaction. This study showed how the ability to self-disclose (which may very likely result in increased trust, enhanced communication skills, and an enduring desire to be with the person) has a positive impact on relationship quality and duration.

    Though much information was gathered from this study, it was not done without limitations. One of these limitations was sample size. Only 60 participants contributed to the study some of which were not even currently in a romantic relationship. The results could have been three times as supportive of the proposed hypotheses had there been a larger sample size. Another limitation was the amount of survey questions asked. More in depth data and results could have been sought with the use of more questions. Thirdly, this study was limited by the type of data collection used. When conducting a survey, there is no real assurance that the participants are answering honestly or accurately. Therefore, it can be highly likely that the data may be skewed, and in hopefully rare cases, false. Due to this study's form of data collection, participants' relationship backgrounds were not indisputably known. Therefore, future researchers may try this type of research on participants in a setting where their intimate relationship background is known, for example, distributing surveys to various marriage counselors and inquiring that they only be given to married couples. It may also be very beneficial to ask what the participants felt caused them to be in counseling, and what they would like to do to try and mend their relationship.

    This research stresses the importance of the ability and willingness to self-disclose and encourages positive interaction as a way to achieve relationship satisfaction. It has continued to

Discussion section of sample research paper, rough draft. From course research paper by Naiara Arozamena, 2007. Copyright 2007 by Naiara Arozamena. Adapted with permission.

FIGURE 6.7 *(Continued)*

VALUE OF PHYSICAL INTERACTION   4

solidify the importance of this type of interaction along with previous research, and has also shown that the quality of interaction in a romantic relationship plays a larger toll on satisfaction than does quantity of interaction. This data is important to consider when pursuing a romantic relationship, and hopefully will shed light onto couples struggling with the question, which aspect of interaction is the most important, the quality or quantity?

Discussion section of sample research paper, rough draft. From course research paper by Naiara Arozamena, 2007. Copyright 2007 by Naiara Arozamena. Adapted with permission.

FIGURE 6.8

VALUE OF PHYSICAL INTERACTION

1 *This will not be page 1 in the final complete draft.*

Discussion

Both the quality and quantity of physical interaction ~~were previously stated~~ *are believed* to be

important to a romantic relationship. However, in this study, the more a couple self-disclosed and

increased the quality of interaction in their intimate relationship, the higher the value,

satisfaction, and intimacy of the relationship as a whole. Noticeably more support was found for

the significance of quality in a relationship than the quantity. The ability to be able to open up,

self-disclose, and be vulnerable with a partner has been shown to increase interaction in general. *avoid passive voice*

good [In other words, being able to let one's guard down and truly make the time with one's partner ~~as rich and fulfilling as it can be~~ may in many cases make the desire and need for interaction greater

and greater.

Both of ~~the~~ *my* predicted hypotheses ~~stated in this research~~ were supported by the data. In

support of the first hypothesis, the increase in the quality of interaction positively influences

relationship intimacy, significant gender differences were found for survey questions regarding

intimate relationship status and frequency of interaction. In both cases, females were more likely

to think of themselves as being in an intimate relationship, as well as feeling that they ~~have more~~ *interact more*

frequent ~~interaction~~ with their partner than ~~the~~ males ~~do~~. This means that the personal definitions

of "intimate relationship" and "interaction" are different for men and women. Also in support of

this hypothesis, a significant correlation was found when examining ~~the~~ *answers to the* survey item "Sharing

personal thoughts, feelings and experiences with my partner increases the quality of our

relationship" and comparing it with the results from *the* item "The more positive interaction I have

with my partner, the more intimate our relationship becomes." In this case, the significant

positive correlation ~~of these two items~~ solidifies that sharing personal thoughts, feelings and

experiences would not only enhance the quality of the relationship, but would also positively

Discussion section of sample research paper with instructor's editing marks. From course research paper by Naiara Arozamena, 2007. Copyright 2007 by Naiara Arozamena. Adapted with permission.

FIGURE 6.8 (*Continued*)

VALUE OF PHYSICAL INTERACTION   2

affect relationship intimacy. This means that, as predicted, the increase of interaction quality in a

relationship tends to lead to an increase in overall interaction and intimacy.

In support of the second hypothesis, the ability to self-disclose positively increases the

quality of a relationship, the item "I feel that I can self-disclose and open up to my partner" ~~was~~ [*answers to*] [*were*]

significantly correlated with "Sharing...with my partner increases relationship quality." ~~This~~ [*responses to*] [*I believe that this outcome means*]

~~positive correlation indicates~~ that the ability and comfort of a partner to self-disclose will lead to

a higher quality relationship. This second hypothesis may also be supported by some of the

results which supported the first hypothesis.

The purpose of Meeks[*, the*] ~~Hendrick, and Hendrick's~~ [*et al.*] (1998) study "was to develop a more

comprehensive perspective on the associations among several conceptually related constructs

and relationship satisfaction" (p. 762). They ~~found~~ [*reported*] that constructs such as conflict tactics, self-

disclosure, and perspective taking were correlated with satisfaction in romantic relationships.

Similarly, ~~the current research was used to and did~~ [*I*] [*found*] that relationship interaction quality

(which was found to be increased by self-disclosure) is more significant to a romantic

relationship than interaction quantity. This finding was also supported by Emmers-Sommer

(2004)[*, in that*] "contact frequency is not necessarily mandatory for a close relationship" (p. 408). ~~Also,~~

~~the current study proposes that self-disclosure is in itself, a very personal form of interaction~~

~~between partners. Previous research has agreed by stating, "Self-disclosing is termed an~~

~~interactional event because it is assumed that sharing such information, in a dyadic situation,~~

~~requires the participation of two willing partners and is likely to affect both of them and the~~

~~relationship between them (Arliss, 1991).~~ [*I believe that*] ~~The~~ he results of this study may have only filled a small

gap that was left by previous studies; however, ~~they~~ [*my findings*] also placed a larger emphasis on the

importance of quality interaction in a romantic relationship.

Discussion section of sample research paper with instructor's editing marks. From course research paper by Naiara Arozamena, 2007. Copyright 2007 by Naiara Arozamena. Adapted with permission.

FIGURE 6.8 (Continued)

VALUE OF PHYSICAL INTERACTION   3

Based on the results of this study, one can speculate that positive, quality time two people spend together in a romantic relationship is not only more important that the amount of time they spend, it is also essential for growth, happiness, and overall relationship satisfaction. This study showed how the ability to self-disclose (which may very likely result in increased trust, enhanced communication skills, and an enduring desire to be with the person) has a positive impact on relationship quality and duration.

Though much information was gathered from this study, it was not done without limitations. One of these limitations was sample size. Only 60 participants contributed to the study, some of which were not even currently in a romantic relationship. The results could have been three times as supportive of the proposed hypotheses had there been a larger sample size. Another limitation was the amount of survey questions asked. More in depth data and results could have been sought with the use of more questions. Thirdly, this study was limited by the type of data collection used. When conducting a survey, there is no real assurance that the participants are answering honestly or accurately. Therefore, it can be highly likely that the data may be skewed, and in hopefully rare cases, false. Due to this study's form of data collection, participants' relationship backgrounds were not indisputably known. Therefore, future researchers may try this type of research on participants in a setting where their intimate relationship background is known; for example, distributing surveys to various marriage counselors and inquiring that they only be given to married couples. It may also be very beneficial to ask what the participants felt caused them to be in counseling, and what they would like to do to try and mend their relationship.

This research stresses the importance of the ability and willingness to self-disclose and encourages positive interaction as a way to achieve relationship satisfaction. It has continued to

Discussion section of sample research paper with instructor's editing marks. From course research paper by Naiara Arozamena, 2007. Copyright 2007 by Naiara Arozamena. Adapted with permission.

FIGURE 6.8 (Continued)

VALUE OF PHYSICAL INTERACTION   4

avoid passive voice solidify the importance of this type of interaction along with previous research, and has also shown that the quality of interaction in a romantic relationship plays a larger toll on satisfaction than does quantity of interaction. This data is important to consider when pursuing a romantic relationship, and hopefully will shed light onto couples struggling with the question, which aspect of interaction is the most important, the quality or quantity?

Discussion section of sample research paper with instructor's editing marks. From course research paper by Naiara Arozamena, 2007. Copyright 2007 by Naiara Arozamena. Adapted with permission.

The Rest of the Story: Title, Abstract, References, and Tables

7

Perhaps the most valuable result of all that education is the ability to make yourself do the thing you have to do, when it ought to be done, whether you like it or not.

—*Thomas Huxley*, Technical Education

In the previous chapter, I covered the sections that make up the bulk of your research paper; however, there are still details to finish before your research paper is complete. Although the title page will be page 1 and the abstract will be page 2, I have students wait until the four main sections of the paper (Introduction, Method, Results, and Discussion) are in draft form before starting on these remaining sections. Why? For one reason: You cannot write an abstract of your study if your study is not complete. Each of these four parts of the manuscript (title page, abstract, references, and tables) are important and have explicit requirements regarding American Psychological Association (APA) format and layout. Below you'll find brief descriptions of each part, with details and examples of how each is prepared. Because I have my students do these parts after writing their Discussion section, I call this assignment TPART.

Titles and Abstracts for Posterity's Sake

Remember that every page is numbered, including the title page. The page numbering appears inside the 1-in. margin, flush right. On the very top line of text, you will provide a running head. What is a running head? Remember that the *Publication Manual* (APA, 2010) is actually a guide for authors submitting their work to journals for possible publication. If you look at an APA journal article, all pages include at the top left of the page a brief phrase—the *running head*—that quickly tells the reader what the article is about. The phrase *Running head:* precedes the running head itself, which appears in all capital letters. This phrase appears on only the title page. The running head appears on all subsequent pages, flush left, on the same line as the page number. In your research paper, this is followed in the horizontal and vertical center of the page by three items, using standard capital and lowercase lettering: (a) the title of your paper; (b) your name; and (c) your affiliation. APA's recommended title length is 10 to 12 words. If you have trouble coming up with a title for your research paper, a generic version of a title is this: "The Effects of the Independent Variable on the Dependent Variable"— just substitute your independent and dependent variables into the generic title. Other typical forms of the title may start with "A Study of . . . ," "An Investigation of . . . ," or "An Experiment on . . ." (Sternberg, 2000).

The title you select is more important than you might think, especially if you continue to write in psychology and writing becomes part of your career. The title is important in capturing the reader's attention, in the article's indexing in databases, and in helping to form first impressions (Sternberg, 2000). Sternberg provided a great example of how a title can provide a positive first impression. A seminal article in cognitive psychology and human memory research is George Miller's (1956) "The Magic Number Seven, Plus or Minus Two: Some Limits on Our Capacity to Process Information." Imagine if that article had been titled "Limitations on Information-Processing Capacity: A Review of the Literature" (Sternberg, 2000, p. 38)!

Your instructor may want your affiliation to be your college or university, or perhaps the course you are enrolled in. Make sure you know what your instructor wants on the title page. Also note that the title-page information is double-spaced—you'll see this in the example that follows, and also in the very helpful sample layout paper starting on page 41 of the *Publication Manual* (APA, 2010).

For new writers of research papers, I think the abstract can be the most difficult section of the paper to write. You have just completed this study demonstrating your comprehension and knowledge of a complex behavioral phenomenon, and now you are asked to condense this massive amount of work into one paragraph that is typically between 150 to 250 words. Writing a coherent abstract is truly an art form, in my opinion. The best way to get a sense of what an abstract should contain is to read them in journal articles and refer to other examples, such as the one in the sample paper here. Your goals in writing your abstract are to be (a) accurate, (b) nonevaluative, (c) coherent and readable, and (d) concise (APA, 2010). In the publication world, the abstract is very important because it becomes part of a database record, which means that it is a key resource when identifying which articles might be relevant, or not relevant, to your research. Prospective readers of your work will read your title first, and then, if it sounds interesting, the abstract second (Sternberg, 2000). However, your instructor will be reading your work no matter what! You will rely on abstracts when you are reading articles and making decisions on whether to extract information using the notecard method (or your variation), and the abstract may help you determine that the article is not as relevant as you may have hoped.

The abstract starts at the top of page 2 in the manuscript, with the word *Abstract* centered on that top line. The abstract is one paragraph long, not indented, and as per APA format, typically ranges between 150 to 250 words. Use the word-count feature of your word-processing program to determine the number of words in your abstract. Will your instructor actually count the words? Probably not, but he or she will have a good idea whether the abstract is too long just by looking at it on the page. Also, when referring to numbers in the abstract, use the actual numerals (5 or 7) rather than spelling them out (*five* or *seven*). The under-10 rule does not apply in abstracts.

References: Your Paper's Pedigree

In other sections of this book, I've already presented details about the preparation of reference material in APA format; here, however, I discuss the preparation of your reference list, which immediately follows your Discussion section. The Reference section starts on its own page and, as is the rest of the paper, the Reference section is also double spaced. A reference list is different from a Modern Library Association "Works Cited" or "Bibliography" page. In APA format, every reference cited in the research paper must appear in the References section, and every reference in the References section must be cited somewhere in the research paper. The author names and publication years cited in the text must match the References section perfectly. References are presented with a hanging indent, meaning that the first line of the reference is flush left, and every remaining line is indented (you will see this in the sample paper). Note that in Microsoft Word, you can key in a reference in perfect APA format, highlight it, and then go to the Paragraph section, Indentation, Special, and you will find the hanging indent option.

As mentioned earlier, your References section is very important. It shows your academic achievement in completing your research paper; as Smith (2000) stated, the task of preparing citations and references "is, however, one of the most important topics regarding manuscript preparation because through citations and references you make or break your reputation as a careful and thorough scholar" (p. 146). The references you list provide the reader with the trail of your scientific and psychological thought processes. Inclusion of seminal works means that you became familiar enough with the literature to know what is important and what is not, which is a characteristic of a developing scholar. In addition, the References section will test your attention to detail because, as previously noted, the rules for presenting reference material in APA format are quite precise. To this end, there are software programs (e.g., EndNote Plus, WPCitation, and Manuscript Manager) that aid in the bibliographic gathering of reference materials; some programs also aid in the formatting of research papers or manuscripts. I think these types of programs are fine in helping you track and organize bibliographic citations; however, I would caution you not to use them in manuscript preparation.

Why? First, if you let a computer program do the APA formatting of your references in text and in the References section, then you won't learn the details yourself (in a similar fashion, children are taught to do math by hand before they are given a calculator). Second, if your instructor deviates from APA style, odds are you cannot tell the program to follow some APA format rules and not others. I recommend that you conquer APA formatting of references on your own first, and then if you want to, rely on a computer program to ease the workload.

Tables at a Glance

In the research paper assignment I give to students, I have them create at least one table so that they can practice formatting a table in APA format. There are many good examples of tables in the *Publication Manual*. In an APA-formatted table, text can be single- or double-spaced, and the table contains no vertical rules (lines)—only horizontal rules are used for clarity. The *Note* at the end of the table often explains the source of the data in the table or the scales or measures used. The benefit of tables is that complex information can be presented in an efficient manner and in a relatively small amount of space (as compared with presenting the same information in repetitive sentences).

How do you determine when to use a table? It was easy for Naiara in my research methods class because I required it as part of the assignment. But if you are left to make the decision yourself, how do you decide? Basically, it comes down to our theme of storytelling. Sometimes a table can be quite efficient at telling a complex story. For example, if you want to demonstrate the complexity between variables (say with a significant interaction), showing the patterns of means and standard deviations in a table can be much more efficient than writing it out in your Results section. However, if you want to show the means and standard deviations of a one-way analysis of variance with three levels, a table is not really necessary; that information is easily (and more efficiently) presented in text. How do you decide? You need to determine which approach better tells the story. Your confidence in this decision will develop over time, but if you have questions, ask a psychology faculty member or consult your local writing center for advice. Figure 7.1 presents each section of Naiara's first draft; Figure 7.2 presents my marked-up version.

Putting It All Together

Consult Figure 7.3 (pp. 147–148) for a mini-checklist of items to consider when preparing the final draft of your research paper.

Sample Research Paper, Completed

I end this chapter with Naiara's completed final version of her research methods paper (Figure 7.4). As I stated earlier, my goal is to present you with real examples of a first rough draft, an edited and marked-up copy, and a final draft. I am not presenting you with a perfect paper. The editorial marks are not perfect, nor is the final draft. You and your instructor will find things that I missed. This is the imperfect nature of teaching and learning. Although Naiara started with a good rough draft, the final draft shows marked improvement. This represents the process of learning and skill attainment—perseverance at an unfamiliar task can lead to your continuous improvement of your scientific writing abilities.

FIGURE 7.1

Running head: VALUE OF PHYSICAL INTERACTION

The Value of Physical Interaction

in a Romantic Relationship

Naiara E. Arozamena

Boise State University

Sample title page, rough draft. From course literature review by Naiara Arozamena, 2007. Copyright 2007 by Naiara Arozamena. Reprinted with permission.

FIGURE 7.1 (*Continued*)

Abstract

The present research examined the importance and value of both the quality and the quantity of physical interaction in a romantic relationship. Individuals were given a survey questioning their personal opinions on intimate relationship interaction. A total of 60 participants took part in the study. The results indicated that there was a significant correlation between couples' ability to self-disclose and their overall relationship quality and satisfaction. There was also a significant difference between males and females regarding intimate relationship status and frequency of interaction with their partners. This suggested that females considered intimacy and interaction differently than males. The significance of interaction in an intimate relationship was discussed, and the differentiation between the importance of the quality and quantity of interaction was presented.

Sample abstract, rough draft. From course literature review by Naiara Arozamena, 2007. Copyright 2007 by Naiara Arozamena. Reprinted with permission.

FIGURE 7.1 *(Continued)*

References

Arliss, L. P. (1991). *Gender communication*. Englewood Cliffs, NJ: Prentice Hall.

Byers, E. S. (2005). Relationship satisfaction and sexual satisfaction: A longitudinal study of individuals in long-term relationships. *The Journal of Sex Research, 42*, 113-118.

Emmers-Sommer, T. M. (2004). The effect of communication quality and quantity indicators on intimacy and relational satisfaction. *Journal of Social and Personal Relationships, 21*, 399-411.

Galliher, R. V., Welsh, D. P., Rostosky, S. S., & Kawaguchi, M. C. (2004). Interaction and relationship quality in late adolescent romantic couples. *Journal of Social and Personal Relationships, 21*, 203-216.

Meeks, B. S., Hendrick, S. S., & Hendrick, C. (1998). Communication, love and relationship satisfaction. *Journal of Social and Personal Relationships, 15*, 755-773.

Tucker, J. S., & Anders, S. L. (1999). Attachment style, interpersonal perception accuracy, and relationship satisfaction in dating couples. *Personality and Social Psychology Bulletin, 25*, 403-412.

Sample reference list, rough draft. From course literature review by Naiara Arozamena, 2007. Copyright 2007 by Naiara Arozamena. Reprinted with permission.

FIGURE 7.1 (*Continued*)

Table 1

Overall Means and Standard Deviations of Survey Items

Items	M	SD
1. I physically interact with my partner _____.	1.72	1.06
2. The more positive interaction I have with my partner, the more intimate our relationship becomes.	4.05	.71
3. I am currently in an intimate relationship.	3.18	1.54
4. I feel that I can self-disclose and open up to my partner.	3.98	.81
5. Sharing personal thoughts, feelings, and experiences with my partner increases the quality of our relationship.	4.24	.64
6. Over the duration of my relationship, our physical interaction has increased.		
7. The frequency of physical interaction is _____ important as the quality of physical interaction.		
8. Duration of present relationship (in years and months)	14.15	18.94
9. Gender		
10. Age	20.87	3.14

Note. Item 6 was answered on a dichotomous scale, with 36.7% no and 63.3% yes. Item 7 was answered on a scale of more (14%), less (26%), and equally (60%). Regarding gender there were 51.7% females and 48.3% males.

Sample table, rough draft. From course literature review by Naiara Arozamena, 2007. Copyright 2007 by Naiara Arozamena. Reprinted with permission.

FIGURE 7.2

Running head: VALUE OF PHYSICAL INTERACTION   1

The Value of Physical Interaction in a Romantic Relationship

Naiara E. Arozamena

Boise State University

Good

Sample title page with instructor's editing marks. From course literature review by Naiara Arozamena, 2007. Copyright 2007 by Naiara Arozamena. Adapted with permission.

FIGURE 7.2 (*Continued*)

(Running head:) VALUE OF PHYSICAL INTERACTION   2

This only appears on p. 1

Abstract

~~The present research~~ examined the importance and value of both the quality and the quantity of
physical interaction in a romantic relationship. Individuals (were given) a survey questioning their *avoid passive voice*
personal opinions on intimate relationship interaction. A total of 60 participants ~~took part in~~ the *completed*
study. ~~The results indicated that~~ there was a significant correlation between couples' ability to *results do not indicate / pos or neg?*
self-disclose and their overall relationship quality and satisfaction. There was also a significant
difference between males and females regarding intimate relationship status and frequency of
interaction with their partners. ~~This~~ suggested that females considered intimacy and interaction
differently than males. The significance of interaction in an intimate relationship ~~was~~ *is* discussed,
and the differentiation between the importance of the quality and quantity of interaction ~~was~~ *is*
emphasized ~~presented.~~

FIGURE 7.2 (Continued)

Running head: VALUE OF PHYSICAL INTERACTION   3

References —center this

Arliss, L. P. (1991). *Gender communication*. Englewood Cliffs, NJ: Prentice Hall.

Byers, E. S. (2005). Relationship satisfaction and sexual satisfaction: A longitudinal study of
lower case
individuals in long-term relationships. *The Journal Of Sex Research, 42*, 113-118.

Emmers-Sommer, T. M. (2004). The effect of communication quality and quantity indicators on

intimacy and relational satisfaction. *Journal of Social and Personal Relationships, 21*,

399-411.

Galliher, R. V., Welsh, D. P., Rostosky, S. S., and Kawaguchi, M. C. (2004). Interaction and

relationship quality in late adolescent romantic couples. *Journal of Social and Personal*

Relationships, 21, 203-216.

Meeks, B. S., Hendrick, S. S., & Hendrick, C. (1998). Communication, love and relationship

satisfaction. *Journal of Social and Personal Relationships, 15*(X), 755-773.

Tucker, J. S., & Anders, S. L. (1999). Attachment Style, Interpersonal Perception Accuracy, and
lower case
Relationship Satisfaction in Dating Couples. *Personality and Social Psychology Bulletin,*

25, 403-412.

Sample reference list with instructor's editing marks. From course literature review by Naiara Arozamena, 2007. Copyright 2007 by Naiara Arozamena. Adapted with permission.

FIGURE 7.2 (*Continued*)

~~Running head:~~ VALUE OF PHYSICAL INTERACTION   4

Table 1

Overall Means and Standard Deviations of Survey Items

Items	M	SD
1. I physically interact with my partner _____.	1.72	1.06
2. The more positive interaction I have with my partner, the more intimate our relationship becomes.	4.05	.71
3. I am currently in an intimate relationship.	3.18	1.54
4. I feel that I can self-disclose and open up to my partner.	3.98	.81
5. Sharing personal thoughts, feelings, and experiences with my partner increases the quality of our relationship.	4.24	.64
6. Over the duration of my relationship, our physical interaction has increased.		
7. The frequency of physical interaction is _____ important as the quality of physical interaction.		
8. Duration of present relationship (in years and months)	14.15	18.94

Note. Item 6 was answered on a dichotomous scale, with 36.7% no and 63.3% yes. Item 7 was answered on a scale of more (14%), less (26%), and equally (60%).

The table should only have 3 horizontal lines and No vertical lines. It is unclear what the scale is for Items 1-5 – be sure to include those details in the table note.

Sample table with instructor's editing marks. From course literature review by Naiara Arozamena, 2007. Copyright 2007 by Naiara Arozamena. Adapted with permission.

FIGURE 7.2 (*Continued*)

Give the scale items 1-5 were measured on.

Note. Item 6 was answered on a dichotomous scale, with 36.7% no and 63.3% yes. Item 7

was answered on a scale of more (14%), less (26%), and equally (60%). Regarding

gender there were 51.7% females and 48.3% males.

Sample table with instructor's editing marks. From course literature review by Naiara Arozamena, 2007. Copyright 2007 by Naiara Arozamena. Reprinted with permission.

FIGURE 7.3

General Formatting and Typing

☐ There are 1-in. (2.54-cm) margins on all four sides of each page of the manuscript.

☐ The typeface is the correct size (12 points on a word processor) and the correct style (serif typeface, such as Courier or Times Roman).

☐ The manuscript is double-spaced throughout, including title page, references, tables, figure captions, and appendixes.

☐ The running head is an abbreviated title.

☐ The page number appears (a) on the same line with the running head. Use the automatic functions of your word-processing program to generate running heads and page numbers.

☐ The running head and page number should appear at the top of each page of the manuscript (except pages containing figures).

☐ There is only one space after most punctuation marks including, commas, colons, semicolons, periods in citations, and all periods in the References section. One or two spaces at the end of sentences is acceptable.

☐ Lowercase letters in parentheses have been used to indicate a series of events or items within a paragraph.

☐ Words are not broken (hyphenated) at the end of a line.

☐ All units of measurement have been correctly abbreviated.

☐ Arabic numerals have been used correctly to express

    ☐ All numbers in the abstract;

    ☐ Numbers that are greater than 10;

    ☐ Numbers that immediately precede a unit of measurement;

    ☐ Numbers that represent fractions and percentages; and

    ☐ Numbers that represent times, dates, ages, samples, populations, scores, or points on a scale.

☐ Words have been correctly used to express

    ☐ Numbers less than 10; and

    ☐ Numbers at the beginning of a title, sentence, or heading.

Final draft checklist. From "A Modified Presubmission Checklist," by J. Dunn, K. Ford, K. L. Rewey, J. A. Juve, A. Weiser, and S. F. Davis, 2001, *Psi Chi Journal of Undergraduate Research, 6,* pp. 142–144. Copyright 2001 by Psi Chi. Adapted with permission.

FIGURE 7.3 *(Continued)*

Title Page

☐ The running head is aligned with the left margin and is equal to or less than 50 characters and spaces long.

Abstract

☐ The word *Abstract* is placed at the top of the page.

☐ The first line of the abstract is even with the left margin.

☐ The abstract typically ranges from 150 to 200 words.

Body of the Manuscript

☐ There are *no* one-sentence paragraphs.

☐ Gender-inclusive language is used through plural pronouns (e.g., *they, their*), by using nouns (e.g., *one, an individual, participant's*), sparse use of *he or she* or *she or he,* or by sparse use of alternating between gendered pronouns (e.g., *he . . . she . . .*).

☐ The words *male* and *female* are used only as adjectives when referring to humans (e.g., female participant), whereas the words *men, women, boys,* and *girls* are used as nouns.

☐ Quotations are word-for-word accurate and page numbers are provided.

☐ The word *while* is used *only* to indicate events that take place simultaneously (alternatives: *although, whereas, and, but*).

☐ The word *since* is used *only* to indicate the passage of time (alternative: *because*).

☐ Terms that are abbreviated are written out completely the first time they are used, then always abbreviated thereafter.

☐ Latin abbreviations are used sparingly and only within parentheses.

☐ The word *and* is used in citations outside of parentheses.

☐ The ampersand (&) is used in citations within parentheses.

☐ When two or more citations are in parentheses, the citations are listed in the same order they appear in the References section.

☐ Each and every citation used in the manuscript is included in the References section.

☐ The phrase *et al.* is used with each citation that lists six or more authors and with each citation that lists three to five authors after the first instance of that citation.

☐ In the Method section, use of the general terms *participants* and *subjects* is acceptable.

☐ In the Results section, all test statistics (e.g., F, t, p) are italicized.

Final draft checklist. From "A Modified Presubmission Checklist," by J. Dunn, K. Ford, K. L. Rewey, J. A. Juve, A. Weiser, and S. F. Davis, 2001, *Psi Chi Journal of Undergraduate Research, 6,* pp. 142–144. Copyright 2001 by Psi Chi. Adapted with permission.

FIGURE 7.3 *(Continued)*

References Section

☐ All entries are listed in alphabetical order.

☐ Each and every entry occurs in the body of the manuscript.

☐ Authors' names are separated by commas.

☐ The volume numbers of journals are italicized.

☐ Each entry is in "hanging indent" format, meaning that the first line of each reference is flush left and every line after the first line of each entry is indented.

☐ The names of journals, book chapters, and books are correctly capitalized.

Final draft checklist. From "A Modified Presubmission Checklist," by J. Dunn, K. Ford, K. L. Rewey, J. A. Juve, A. Weiser, and S. F. Davis, 2001, *Psi Chi Journal of Undergraduate Research, 6,* pp. 142–144. Copyright 2001 by Psi Chi. Adapted with permission.

FIGURE 7.4

Running Head: VALUE OF PHYSICAL INTERACTION   1

The Value of Physical Interaction in a Romantic Relationship

Naiara E. Arozamena

Boise State University

Complete sample research paper, final draft. From course literature review by Naiara Arozamena, 2007. Copyright 2007 by Naiara Arozamena. Adapted with permission.

FIGURE 7.4 *(Continued)*

VALUE OF PHYSICAL INTERACTION   2

                                    Abstract

The present research examined the importance and value of both the quality and the quantity of

physical interaction in a romantic relationship. Individuals ($N = 60$) received a survey

questioning their personal opinions on intimate relationship interaction. The results indicate that

there is a significant positive correlation between couples' ability to self-disclose and their

overall relationship quality and satisfaction. There is also a significant difference between

males' and females' perceptions regarding intimate relationship status and frequency of

interaction with their partners. This suggests that females considered intimacy and interaction

differently than males. The importance of interacting in an intimate relationship is discussed, and

the differentiation between the quality and quantity of interaction is highlighted.

FIGURE 7.4 (*Continued*)

VALUE OF PHYSICAL INTERACTION   3

The Value of Physical Interaction in a Romantic Relationship

That first smile, the first look of compassion and care, the first soft touch after a compliment given, the first long gaze, every first interaction with someone new that brings about a feeling of joy and excitement. Humans yearn for a feeling of intimacy and connection with one another because it is in our nature. People with a romantic partner are able to understand the true magnitude of interaction. These experiences are why the quantity and quality of physical interaction are such vital parts of maintaining a romantic relationship. Previous researchers such as Emmers-Sommer (2004) may have recognized and stressed the importance of interaction in brief, however, the question here is—which aspect of interaction is the most important, the quality or quantity?

Many couples want a successful relationship that is also satisfying. Partners who are satisfied with their interactions tend to be satisfied with other, non-romantic relationships (Emmers-Sommer, 2004). In order to reach this satisfaction, one might speculate that interactions between partners needed to be both frequent and fulfilling. As a response to ongoing interaction between partners, loving attitudes are formed, which are shaped by personality type and past and existing relationship interactions (Meeks, Hendrick, & Hendrick, 1998). These love attitudes are also factors in determining relationship satisfaction. Poor communication results in decreased satisfaction in a number of areas of relationship functioning, including sexual satisfaction and overall relationship satisfaction (Byers, 2005). Having recurrent interactions with a partner would allow for an abundance of occasions to learn about the person and over time decide personal relationship satisfaction. However, one might feel that the quality of the interaction, even though possibly brief, eventually determines this same romantic relationship

Complete sample research paper, final draft. From course literature review by Naiara Arozamena, 2007. Copyright 2007 by Naiara Arozamena. Adapted with permission.

FIGURE 7.4 (*Continued*)

VALUE OF PHYSICAL INTERACTION   4

satisfaction. Either way, people interact when they are doing things together, and doing things

together usually results in positive relational experiences (Emmers-Sommer, 2004).

So which aspect of interaction in a relationship is more important, the amount of

interaction, or the quality of it? Arguments for both sides exist. For example, Emmers-Sommer

(2004) found that contact frequency is not necessarily mandatory for a close relationship, but that

frequency of in-person contact is significant in relational satisfaction. Self-disclosure defined as

face-to-face communication of personal information is often reciprocal, therefore related to the

development of close personal ties (Arliss, 1991). Another aspect to examine is if males and

females view interaction and relationship quality differently, as suggested by Galliher, Welsh,

Rostosky and Kawaguchi (2004): "the domains of couple interaction that predict global

relationship quality were different for males and females" (p. 214). Tucker and Anders (1999)

also found that women may be more satisfied when their partner shows concern with emotional

intimacy, but the same may not be true of men. Two partners might not be able to fully self-

disclose without being in proximity of one another, with important eye-contact and physical

presence. This difference of opinion results in a knowledge gap about the relative importance of

each of these aspects of interaction.

The goal of this study is to inspect and evaluate the differences and importance of the

quality and quantity of physical interaction in a heterosexual romantic relationship. The method

of research for this study will be the distribution of a survey to undergraduate PSYC 101 students

at Boise State University. The presence of an intimate relationship will be inquired as well as the

duration. Gender and age data will also be collected.

Emerging from the data examined and studied so far are the following proposed

hypotheses: (a) The increase in the quality of interaction positively influences relationship

Complete sample research paper, final draft. From course literature review
by Naiara Arozamena, 2007. Copyright 2007 by Naiara Arozamena.
Adapted with permission.

FIGURE 7.4 *(Continued)*

VALUE OF PHYSICAL INTERACTION   5

intimacy; it is expected that the participants' disclosure on the quality of their relationship

interaction has had a positive effect on their romantic relationship, and (b) the ability to self-

disclose positively increases the quality of a relationship. The importance and results of using

self-disclosure in a romantic relationship will be examined and hopefully support this hypothesis.

Having the ability to open up to someone seems to be a vital and necessary component in

maintaining a healthy and productive relationship.

Method

Participants

For this study, 60 participants from Boise State University were used to help gather the

necessary information. The PSYC 101 students ranged in age from 18 through 30 ($M = 20.87$,

$SD = 3.14$) and were recruited using a program called Experimetrix. The participants consisted

of 28 males and 30 females (two participants did not specify their gender) of all different

relationship statuses (single, divorced, married, engaged, and boyfriend/girlfriend). For those

participants in an intimate relationship, the duration of that relationship was asked for in months

($M = 14.15$, $SD = 18.94$). The participants were selected by their volunteering to participate and

were rewarded with points for their PSYC 101 course.

Materials

Survey questions were developed entirely by the author, based on the hypotheses to be

tested and a review of the literature. The materials were pilot tested. Please refer to Table 1 for

the survey items used.

Procedure

The study was conducted in a large lecture room with participants present, as well as the

author. The questions in Table 1 were a part of a larger survey being administered. The room

Complete sample research paper, final draft. From course literature review by Naiara Arozamena, 2007. Copyright 2007 by Naiara Arozamena. Adapted with permission.

FIGURE 7.4 *(Continued)*

VALUE OF PHYSICAL INTERACTION   6

was quiet, and participants were allotted 60 min to complete the 190 item survey. The survey

was anonymous. Following completion of the survey, participants were debriefed and thanked.

Results

Descriptive Statistics

   Please refer to Table 1 for all the means and standard deviations of the survey items.

Question-by-Question Analyses

   The first hypothesis is that the increase in the quality of interaction positively influences

relationship intimacy. When examining the effects of gender using a t test with the survey item

"I am currently in an intimate relationship" using an agreement scale from 1 (*strongly disagree*)

to 5 (*strongly agree*), there is a significant difference between males ($M = 2.65, SD = 1.38$) and

females ($M = 3.66, SD = 1.58$) on intimate relationship status, $t (54) = -2.530, p < .05$. When

examining the item "I physically interact with my partner" using a frequency scale from 0

(*never*) to 3 (*always*), there is a significant difference between males ($M = 1.29, SD = 1.08$) and

females ($M = 2.17, SD = .88$) on frequency of interaction scores, $t (45) = -3.049, p < .05$. A t test

was also used to examine the relationship between agreement scale item "Sharing personal

thoughts, feelings and experiences with my partner increases the quality of our relationship" and

dichotomous scale 1 (*yes*) and 0 (*no*) item "Over the duration of my relationship, our physical

interaction has increased." A significant difference was found between the participants who

answered "yes" ($M = 4.43, SD = .56$) and those who answered "no" ($M = 3.94, SD = .65$) on self-

disclosure scores, $t (45) = 2.693, p < .05$.

   Of the 54 participants who responded by agreement scale for the item "The more positive

interaction I have with my partner, the more intimate our relationship becomes," 33 answered

agree and 13 answered *strongly agree* (totaling 85.2%), but only eight said *anything less*

Complete sample research paper, final draft. From course literature review
by Naiara Arozamena, 2007. Copyright 2007 by Naiara Arozamena.
Adapted with permission.

FIGURE 7.4 (Continued)

VALUE OF PHYSICAL INTERACTION   7

(14.8%). In support of Hypothesis 1, there is a significant correlation between the item "The more positive interaction, the more intimate," and item "Sharing personal thoughts…increases relationship quality," $r(50) = .465, p < .01$.

The second hypothesis suggests that the ability to self-disclose positively increases the quality of a relationship. This prediction was sustained by the significant correlation between agreement scale item "I feel that I can self-disclose and open up to my partner" and the item "Sharing . . . with my partner increases relationship quality," $r(51) = .733, p < .01$.

Discussion

Both the quality and quantity of physical interaction were previously stated to be important to a romantic relationship. However, in this study, the more a couple self-disclosed and increased the quality of interaction in their intimate relationship, the higher the value, satisfaction, and intimacy of the relationship as a whole. Noticeably more support exists for the significance of quality in a relationship than the quantity. The ability to be able to open up, self-disclose, and be vulnerable with a partner increases interaction in general. In other words, being able to let one's guard down and truly make the time with one's partner as rich and fulfilling as it can be may in many cases make the desire and need for interaction greater.

Both of the predicted hypotheses stated in this research were supported by the data. In support of the first hypothesis, the increase in the quality of interaction positively influences relationship intimacy, significant gender differences exist for survey items regarding intimate relationship status and frequency of interaction. In both cases, females were more likely to think of themselves as being in an intimate relationship, as well as feeling that they have more frequent interaction with their partner than the males do. This means that the personal definitions of "intimate relationship" and "interaction" are different for men and women. Also in support of

Complete sample research paper, final draft. From course literature review by Naiara Arozamena, 2007. Copyright 2007 by Naiara Arozamena. Adapted with permission.

FIGURE 7.4 (*Continued*)

VALUE OF PHYSICAL INTERACTION   8

this hypothesis, a significant correlation exists when examining the survey item "Sharing personal thoughts, feelings and experiences with my partner increases the quality of our relationship" and comparing it with the results from item "The more positive interaction I have with my partner, the more intimate our relationship becomes." In this case, the significant positive correlation of these two items solidifies that sharing personal thoughts, feelings and experiences would not only enhance the quality of the relationship, but would also positively affect relationship intimacy. This means that, as predicted, the increase of interaction quality in a relationship tends to lead to an increase in overall interaction and intimacy.

In support of the second hypothesis, the ability to self-disclose positively increases the quality of a relationship, the item "I feel that I can self-disclose and open up to my partner" was significantly correlated with "Sharing...with my partner increases relationship quality." This positive correlation indicates that the ability and comfort of a partner to self-disclose will lead to a higher quality relationship. This second hypothesis may also be supported by some of the results which supported the first hypothesis.

Meeks et al. (1998) wanted to develop a more comprehensive perspective on the associations among several conceptually related constructs and relationship satisfaction. They found that constructs such as conflict tactics, self-disclosure, and perspective taking were correlated with satisfaction in romantic relationships. Similarly, the current research tested that relationship interaction quality (which was found to be increased by self-disclosure) is more significant to a romantic relationship than interaction quantity. This finding was also supported by Emmers-Sommer (2004) when she explained how contact frequency is not necessarily mandatory for a close relationship. Also, the current study proposes that self-disclosure is in itself, a very personal form of interaction between partners. Arliss (1991) has agreed by stating,

Complete sample research paper, final draft. From course literature review by Naiara Arozamena, 2007. Copyright 2007 by Naiara Arozamena. Adapted with permission.

FIGURE 7.4 (*Continued*)

VALUE OF PHYSICAL INTERACTION 9

"Self-disclosing is termed an interactional event because it is assumed that sharing such information, in a dyadic situation, requires the participation of two willing partners and is likely to affect both of them and the relationship between them" (p. 71). The results of this study fills a gap left by previous studies; however, previous studies placed a larger emphasis on the importance of quality interaction in a romantic relationship.

Based on the results of this study, one can speculate that the positive quality time two people spend together in a romantic relationship is not only more important that the amount of time they spend, it is also essential for growth, happiness, and overall relationship satisfaction. This study demonstrates how the ability to self-disclose (which may very likely result in increased trust, enhanced communication skills, and an enduring desire to be with the person) has a positive impact on relationship quality and duration.

One of the limitations of this study was sample size. Only 60 individuals participated, some of which were not even currently in a romantic relationship. More in-depth data and results could be obtained with more survey items. This study was also limited by the type of data collected. When conducting a survey, there is no real assurance that the participants are answering honestly or accurately. Therefore, the data may be skewed, and in hopefully rare cases, false. Due to this potential threat, participants' relationship backgrounds were not indisputably known. Therefore, future researchers may want to continue this type of research with participants in a setting where an intimate relationship background is known, for example, distributing surveys to marriage counselors to administer to clients and requiring that the survey only be given to married couples. It would be beneficial to ask what the participants believed the cause of seeking counseling, and what they would like to do to mend their relationship.

Complete sample research paper, final draft. From course literature review by Naiara Arozamena, 2007. Copyright 2007 by Naiara Arozamena. Adapted with permission.

FIGURE 7.4 (*Continued*)

VALUE OF PHYSICAL INTERACTION   10

      This research stresses the importance of the ability and willingness to self-disclose and encourages positive interaction as a way to achieve relationship satisfaction. It continues to solidify the importance of this type of interaction along with previous research, and shows that the quality of interaction in a romantic relationship plays an important role in satisfaction. These issues are important to consider when pursuing a romantic relationship, and hopefully this research will shed light onto couples struggling with the question—which aspect of interpersonal interaction is more important, quality or quantity?

Complete sample research paper, final draft. From course literature review **by Naiara** Arozamena, 2007. Copyright 2007 by Naiara Arozamena. **Adapted** with permission.

FIGURE 7.4 *(Continued)*

VALUE OF PHYSICAL INTERACTION   11

References

Arliss, L. P. (1991). *Gender communication*. Englewood Cliffs, NJ: Prentice Hall.

Byers, E. S. (2005). Relationship satisfaction and sexual satisfaction: A longitudinal study of
individuals in long-term relationships. *The Journal of Sex Research, 42*, 113-118.

Emmers-Sommer, T. M. (2004). The effect of communication quality and quantity indicators on
intimacy and relational satisfaction. *Journal of Social and Personal Relationships, 21*,
399-411.

Galliher, R. V., Welsh, D. P., Rostosky, S. S., & Kawaguchi, M. C. (2004). Interaction and
relationship quality in late adolescent romantic couples. *Journal of Social and Personal
Relationships, 21*, 203-216.

Meeks, B. S., Hendrick, S. S., & Hendrick, C. (1998). Communication, love and relationship
satisfaction. *Journal of Social and Personal Relationships, 15*, 755-773.

Tucker, J. S., & Anders, S. L. (1999). Attachment style, interpersonal perception accuracy, and
relationship satisfaction in dating couples. *Personality and Social Psychology Bulletin,
25*, 403-412.

Complete sample research paper, final draft. From course literature review
by Naiara Arozamena, 2007. Copyright 2007 by Naiara Arozamena.
Adapted with permission.

FIGURE 7.4 *(Continued)*

VALUE OF PHYSICAL INTERACTION   12

Table 1

Overall Means and Standard Deviations of Survey Items

Items	M	SD
The more positive interaction I have with my partner, the more intimate our relationship becomes.	4.05	.71
I am currently in an intimate relationship.	3.18	1.54
I feel that I can self-disclose and open up to my partner.	3.98	.81
Sharing personal thoughts, feelings, and experiences with my partner increases the quality of our relationship.	4.24	.64

Note. Above items were answered on an agreement scale from 1 (*strongly disagree*) to 5 (*strongly agree*). An additional item ("Over the duration of my relationship, our physical interaction has increased") was answered on a dichotomous scale, with 36.7% no responses and 63.3% yes responses.

Complete sample research paper, final draft. From course literature review by Naiara Arozamena, 2007. Copyright 2007 by Naiara Arozamena. Adapted with permission.

Reshaping Your Story for Different Audiences: Other Types of Writing in Psychology

8

To me, the greatest pleasure of writing is not what it's about, but the inner music that the words make.

—*Truman Capote*

The vast bulk of this book has been devoted to scientific writing and its many forms in psychology courses. In fact, there are numerous outlets specifically designed for undergraduate students' scientific writing in psychology. There are at least five journals dedicated to publishing undergraduate student research in psychology: *Modern Psychological Studies, The Undergraduate Journal of Psychology,* the *Journal of Psychological Inquiry,* the *Journal of Psychology and the Behavioral Sciences,* and the *Psi Chi Journal of Undergraduate Research* (a simple Google search will send you to the home page of each journal). However, there are other types of scientific writing that I have not discussed until now. This final chapter presents, briefly, other types of writing that you may encounter as an undergraduate student. This is certainly not meant to be an exhaustive list of all the other types of writing you will encounter; here, the specific focus is on (a) writing for oral presentations at conferences, (b) writing for poster presentations at conferences, (c) writing for the Web, (d) writing for an essay exam, and (e) writing for pleasure and insight.

Oral Presentations at Conferences

As an undergraduate student, you may have the opportunity to present the outcomes of a class project or research paper at a conference. Such conferences are held locally (sometimes), statewide, regionally, nationally, and even internationally. An important part of becoming part of the scientific culture is to learn the skills of a scientist. As part of good science, psychologists gather on a frequent basis to share information and present the findings of our latest research. To acculturate students to this environment, many psychology conferences have student sections of the conference during which students participate in the same types of tasks as psychologists, such as giving an oral paper presentation or participating in a poster session.

An oral presentation at a conference usually includes a student speaking to an audience for about 12 to 15 minutes (a conference poster presentation is much different and is covered in the next section). Essentially, you are making an oral presentation to the audience about your research paper or project. Your goal is to give an engaging presentation of the outcomes of your research. The next two paragraphs include suggestions by Karlin (2000), Landrum and Davis (2007), and Langston (2002) on how you should present your talk to the audience.

A safe opening is to read the title of your talk and introduce yourself, and be sure to thank any others who contributed to the project. Do not read your talk, but have notes prepared for every section of it. What sections? A very logical sequence would be Introduction, Method, Results, and Discussion—sound familiar? Remember to speak slowly and clearly, but not in a monotone. You know from listening to your professors who sounds good and who doesn't—try to copy the style of presentation you find most informative. Consider the big picture. What are the main ideas and findings of your study? Decide on a limited number of significant ideas that you want your audience to comprehend and remember.

In chapter 6, I presented a sample paper from my student Naiara. Let's say that she has now decided to present her paper at a conference during an oral presentation session. It would be pretty boring for her audience to sit and listen to her read her paper word for word; a better strategy would be for her to extract the most useful information and tell the audience a compelling story about her research and what she found. Instead of reading the paper's introduction to the audience, her introduction might sound like this:

> Do you remember the first time you fell in love? Remember the intensity of the feelings, and remember how much it hurt when you "broke up" with someone for the first time? Even at a young

age, intimacy plays a large role in shaping the happiness of our future. In the end, we all want a satisfying relationship with a loving, romantic partner that yields deep interactions. But here is my question for you—which is more important, the quality of interactions you have with your partner, or the quantity of interactions you have with your partner? I designed my research to begin to answer this exact question.

By setting up the story in this fashion, audience members should be curious to know how the results turn out. A compelling story carries our attention (Kendall-Tackett, 2007), and for whatever reason, we desire closure, that is, knowing how the story turns out (or in this case, the results of the study).

You should dress nicely—business professional. If it makes sense for your presentation, try to engage the audience in a brief activity related to your study—it's a great way to encourage your audience to be active participants in your talk. Prepare overheads or PowerPoint slides to keep your audience engaged in your presentation. These visual aids should be simple and prepared in such a way that individuals in the back of the room can see them. As a general rule, use nothing smaller than an 18-point font, and a 24-point font is even better. Try to speak loudly and clearly enough to hold your audience's attention. There will be distractions—people coming in, others getting up and leaving. Don't be offended. Try to be enthusiastic enough to sustain interest over these distractions. State your final conclusions and end on time. Be prepared to answer audience questions if time permits. No one will purposely try to stump you with a question at the end of a talk. However, if you do not know the answer, say "I don't know." If you want to speculate, that's okay, but tell the audience that it is only your speculation.

Students who present during a conference experience what it is like to be a scientist sharing his or her results with an audience. Although a bit nerve-racking at first, your 12 to 15 minutes will go by quickly, and the professional experience is invaluable. However, if you are not quite ready to give an oral presentation, but do have research to present at a conference, there is another option, and it is one used by faculty researchers and students alike—the conference poster presentation.

Poster Presentations

A poster presentation is substantially different from a paper presentation. In a paper presentation, you present your findings to an audience in a relatively short time period. The method is somewhat impersonal, but it is an efficient method to present the materials to a large number of people. In a poster presentation, you present your research work in a poster format for a longer period of time (1½–2 hours). You are available to speak personally with "audience members" who are interested in your work. You will probably reach fewer people with a poster session, but you'll have more personal conversations with people who are genuinely interested in your work. Posters are displayed on a free-standing bulletin board in a session with other posters, in a room large enough to hold the posters, the presenters, and the people who wander through the session. The audience members (conference attendees) pick and choose what posters to read; they can acquire more detailed information from the poster authors in this one-on-one conversation format (Landrum & Davis, 2007).

There are a number of resources available to help you design your poster, including valuable tips in this chapter. The Psi Chi Web site (http://www.psichi.org) has nice resources available not only to help students prepare posters but also about the poster presentation during a conference session. You can also find helpful templates for designing posters in PowerPoint at http://office.microsoft.com/en-us/templates/TC100214271033.aspx (you'll see they call it a medical poster or scientific poster—that's us!).

As a general rule, I prefer to prepare a poster from a completed manuscript, such as a research paper. Essentially, the text of the paper becomes the text of the poster, but in a shortened format. The text provided in a poster can only be enough to provide a context for the study. The goal of your poster session is to engage audience members as they stop by to talk. You can provide them with a complete copy of your poster or paper, but the key is conversation. You can learn much about your research and that of others by talking to learned professionals about what you have done. I have often gotten an idea for the next study just by presenting my research at a poster session. Here are some tips for preparing a conference poster (some from Szuchman, 2005) and some mock-ups of how a poster might be designed (Figures 8.1, 8.2, and 8.3; Psi Chi, 2007). Finally, Figure 8.4 displays a sample of a poster I presented with a student coauthor, Toni Hunt.

Construct the poster to include the title, author(s), affiliation(s), and a description of the research. Your poster should be readable from a distance of 3 feet. Posters are true to the spirit of American Psychological Association format, but the rules of presentation are relaxed. Minimize the detail that is presented and try to use jargon-free statements. Pictures, tables, and figures are especially useful and helpful in poster presentations. During your poster presentation, have your name badge on and placed where conference attendees can see it. Be ready to put up and take down your poster at the specified times (you may want to bring your own thumbtacks or pushpins); poster sessions are often scheduled back to back, so you want to end on time so the next session can begin on time. Bring 30 to 50 copies of your handouts to provide more information

FIGURE 8.1

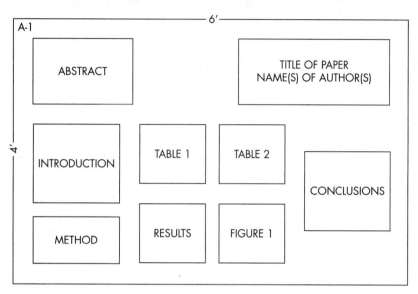

Sample poster layout. From Sample Poster Arrangements by the Western Psychological Association. Retrieved from http://www.psichi.org/conventions/samples.aspx. Copyright 2007 by the Western Psychological Association. Reprinted with permission.

about your study and your contact information. And finally, at a poster session, you may be on your feet for 1½ to 2 hours—wear comfortable shoes! Note that the example poster in Figure 8.4 is text heavy, and probably not the best-designed poster (yes, sometimes I don't practice what I preach). However, this example does show you the various sections you will want to have in any poster presentation.

Writing for the Web

In addition to the more typical outlets for scientific works such as journal articles, books, oral conference presentations, and poster sessions, the World Wide Web (i.e., the Internet) has become a powerful force in communicating scientific information, especially at a rapid rate. Of course, all of the concerns about the accuracy and veracity of information on the Internet still apply, and ensuring the author's credibility is of utmost importance. But the Internet allows for almost worldwide availability

FIGURE 8.2

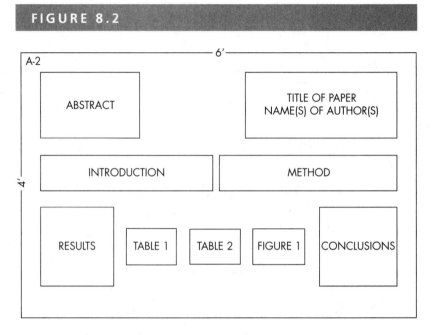

Sample poster layout. From Sample Poster Arrangements
by the Western Psychological Association. Retrieved
from http://www.psichi.org/conventions/samples.aspx.
Copyright 2007 by the Western Psychological Association.
Reprinted with permission.

of information, including valuable scientific information. If your goal is
to communicate the results of your research using this vehicle, there are
some things to know about writing for the Web.

MOST EFFECTIVE DESIGN PRINCIPLES

Although not specifically Web advice, Mayer (2001) has spent much of
his career studying the principles of effective multimedia design. On
the basis of research he and others have conducted, these are the general
principles he has identified as essential for effective multimedia design:

1. Students learn better from words and pictures than from words
   alone.
2. Students learn better when corresponding words and pictures
   are presented near to rather than far from each other on the page
   or screen.
3. Students learn better when corresponding words and pictures
   are presented simultaneously rather than successively.

FIGURE 8.3

Sample poster layout. From Sample Poster Arrangements by the Western Psychological Association. Retrieved from http://www.psichi.org/conventions/samples.aspx. Copyright 2007 by the Western Psychological Association. Reprinted with permission.

4. Students learn better when extraneous words, pictures, and sounds are excluded rather than included.
5. Students learn better from animation and narration than from animation and on-screen text.
6. Students learn better from animation and narration than from animation, narration, and on-screen text.
7. Design effects are stronger for low-knowledge learners than for high-knowledge learners and for high-spatial learners than for low-spatial learners.

Understanding how students learn via information presented on a Web page can certainly help tailor the delivery your the message on the Web. But what about what to write (and how to write it)?

TIPS FOR WRITING FOR THE WEB

You will not be taking the best advantage of the Web as an information delivery medium if you merely cut and paste pages or passages from a

FIGURE 8.4

Providing Lecture Notes to Students: Differing Perceptions of Students and Faculty

Midwestern Psychological Association, Chicago, IL.
May 4, 2006

Toni N. Hunt & R. Eric Landrum
Department of Psychology

Abstract

A fusion of ideas and opinions between instructional staff and students is important for a more meaningful and productive academic relationship. By looking at the opinions of both instructional staff and students, one can see the differences in opinion and thus the areas in need of revision. There were four areas found to contain differences between the instructional staff's and student's opinion. Two areas where the students agreed with the statements significantly more than this instructional staff were: the preference of notes before class, and the overall grading increased with the provision of notes before class. The instructional staff agreed more specifically on two differing points of overall grade average is not affected by lecture notes given before class, and the provision of notes to students before class has no affect on student's attendance. These differing opinions indicate a need for further adaptation in student and instructional needs as well as a need for further study.

Cooperation and communication are vital between university instructional staff and undergraduate students to establish and maintain successful academic relationships. A key component in nourishing this relationship is a mutual understanding of the needs and materials desired by both parties. To our knowledge, not much research has been conducted in examining faculty and student differences in the expectation of the provision of course materials, and in particular, the provision of lecture notes to students. Some research deals with minority students (Dovey, 1997; Zhang, 2000) or specific criteria, such as student based interactions (Fowler, 2001; Metzger, 2003). These types of studies concentrate more student factors such as race and personal issues such as attitudes towards subject matter and perceptions of the learning environment. This study focuses specifically on the preparedness of both the students and instructors and compares the preferences of both. It concentrates primarily on three factors: (a) expectations of faculty and students for faculty to provide lecture notes to students, (b) faculty and student perceptions concerning how grades and attendance may be affected by the distribution of lecture notes; and (c) faculty and student perceptions of how lecture note policies may influence student attendance.

Method

There were 76 undergraduate students and 47 full-time instructors from Boise State University that participated in this study. The students participated as part of fulfilling a research experience requirement. A random sample of 200 full-time instructors were requested to participate in the instructor portion of this project; 47 (23.5%) completed an online survey similar to the student survey.

The survey instrument was a compilation of questions we generated, and response scales including agreement, frequency, open-ended items. The student study was conducted using our PSYC 101 General Psychology subject pool; students were tested in one group in a classroom. The instructor survey was nearly identical to that of the student version; faculty members were emailed with an invitation to participate in the online survey and were provided with a URL link to participate.

Results

The Provision of Lecture Notes

These survey items were answered on an agreement scale (1 = strongly disagree to 5 = strongly agree). There was a significant difference between students ($M = 3.96$, $SD = 0.9$) and faculty ($M = 2.64$, $SD = 1.1$) on responses to the item "I believe that instructors should provide lecture notes to students prior to the class session," $t(121) = -6.77$, $p < .001$. There was not a significant difference between students ($M = 3.93$, $SD = 0.8$) and faculty ($M = 4.09$, $SD = 1.0$) on responses to the item "I expect students to take notes in my class," $t(120) = 0.87$, n.s.

Lecture Notes and Grades

These survey items were answered on an agreement scale (1 = strongly disagree to 5 = strongly agree). There was a significant difference between students ($M = 3.54$, $SD = 0.8$) and faculty ($M = 2.72$, $SD = 0.9$) on responses to the item "Overall class grade averages increase with the provision of lecture notes before class," $t(116) = -5.15$, $p < .001$. There was a significant difference between students ($M = 2.61$, $SD = 0.8$) and faculty ($M = 2.98$, $SD = 1.0$) on responses to the item "Overall class grade averages are not affected with the provision of notes before class," $t(120) = 2.26$, $p < .05$.

Lecture Notes and Attendance

These survey items were answered on an agreement scale (1 = strongly disagree to 5 = strongly agree). There was not a significant difference between students ($M = 2.23$, $SD = 0.8$) and faculty ($M = 2.30$, $SD = 0.8$) on responses to the item "Withholding personal notes encourages students to skip class," $t(118) = 0.46$, n.s. There was a significant difference between students ($M = 2.29$, $SD = 0.9$) and faculty ($M = 2.87$, $SD = 1.0$) on responses to the item "Providing notes to students before class has no effect on student attendance," $t(119) = 3.21$, $p < .005$.

Discussion

The results for the first area of interest indicates that the students have a higher preference for having class notes before class begins, whereas instructional staff have a lesser preference for the giving of said notes. This would indicate an area to be worked on between the two parties. However, in this same portion of study on provision of lecture notes, the two parties are in agreement on the opinion concerning the expectation that students should take notes in class where both agree to this statement.

In the second area, there were two items analyzed. The first variable (overall class grade averages increase with the provision of lecture notes before class) was an area of difference for the two groups. The instructional staff on average tended to disagree with this statement more than the students did. The second factor (overall class grade averages are not affected with the provision of notes before class) was also a matter of dissimilarity where the instructional staff tended to agree more with the statement then the students. It is interesting to note on this factor, however, that the average instructional staff's response is very close to the number indicating a neutral response. So, in this case the student's tendency to disagree with the statement was coupled with a neutral stance from the instructional staff.

The last topic studied concerned lecture notes and attendance. "Withholding personal notes encourages students to skip class" was the first item analyzed. The instructional staff agreed more with this statement than the students, but not significantly. The difference in lecture notes and attendance came with the second variable, "providing notes to students before class has no effect on student attendance." Overall, the students disagreed with this statement more than the instructional staff did. Continued work in this area should include a more thorough analysis of the matches and mismatches between student and faculty expectations.

Example of poster at session.

Microsoft Word document to a Web page. Writing for the Web is different from writing for print, as Gerry McGovern (n.d.) points out:

> . . . people behave differently when online. When viewing a new page, they don't read—they scan. They look at headings and subheadings first; they scan for hyperlinks, numerals, and keywords. They jump around, scrolling and clicking—their fingers never far from the browser's "Back" button. (para. 4)

Three strategies to use in writing for the Web are (a) be as brief as possible; (b) be direct and make information easy to find; and (c) write for scanning by guiding the reader with headings, subheadings, and font and layout/design choices (McGovern, n.d.).

Similar to preparing your work for a scientific writing assignment, numerous tips are available to help you prepare for writing on the Web. Some suggestions from Jupitermedia Corporation (2001) are to use action verbs to engage readers and catch readers' attention and draw them in. Be descriptive and offer an accurate depiction of what they will get if they read further, and be yourself and write conversationally (storytelling!).

Chunk information into bite-sized bits (remember that Web readers may not read your pages in order, so make each page stand-alone so that it can be read out of order). Spell-check your work, but go beyond reliance on your spell-checker only. There are many additional resources you can consult, on the Web or in print, if you intend to do substantial writing in this relatively new medium.

Writing for the Web presents many opportunities for students and for faculty (Myers, 2007). In addition to posting research reports or datasets on the Internet, you can use the Web to target a specific audience or tell a specific story. During an internship, you might be asked to help create Web pages for the advocacy group you are working for, or you may be posting fact sheets or self-quizzes to help raise awareness. Writing for the Web benefits from all the general practices I have covered, such as writing for your audience and telling a compelling story. Many talented individuals post valuable information on the Web; if you have any doubts about that, take a peek at the References section at the back of this book.

Essay Exams

Writing for an essay exam is different from any other type of writing discussed thus far. It is a very time-intensive and anxiety-provoking task for students because of the demands of recall memory and the challenge of coherently answering the specific question that is asked. The tips in the sections below are combined from Landrum and Davis (2007) and the University of Texas Learning Center (2006).

BEFORE YOU WRITE

Time is usually a critical factor in an essay exam. When reviewing questions, consider what you know, the time you think it will take to answer, and each question's point value. Read all the essay questions before you start to write. As you read the questions, underline key words (e.g., *compare, explain, justify,* and *define*). Answer the questions that you know first, but don't neglect questions with high point values. Begin with the question that seems easiest to you. By doing this, you reduce anxiety, build confidence, and facilitate clear thinking. Before actually writing, jot a rough outline on your test answer sheet: List quickly, as they come to you, as many ideas and facts as you can remember. Number your points in the order in which you want to present them, discriminating main issues and supporting details and examples. If, as you are writing the answer to one question, you think of ideas and examples that you can apply to other questions, jot them down on the test answer sheet so you won't forget them.

WHILE YOU WRITE

The challenge with essays is to be both complete and concise. Avoid the "kitchen-sink" method (you don't know the exact answer, so you write all you know hoping the answer is in there somewhere). That is, come up with a definite, clear sentence that directly answers the question. If possible, leave space for additions to your answer by writing on every other line and on only one side of each page. You've probably learned a great deal of jargon and terminology in the course, so demonstrate what you've learned in your essay. Be sure to write legibly. When you reach the end of your allotted time period for a given question, move on to the next item; partially answering all questions is better than fully answering some but not answering others. The instructor can't give you any credit for a question you haven't attempted. If you don't know much about a question, relax and brainstorm for a few moments about the topic. Recall pages from your texts, particular lectures, and class discussions to trigger your memory about ideas relevant to the question. Write these ideas down as coherently as you can. And finally, if your mind goes blank, relax: Take some slow, deep breaths, and just for a moment, think about something pleasant that's unrelated to the test. Then, let your mind recall through association or redirect your attention to a different question.

AFTER YOU WRITE

Time permitting, reread your answers and make any additions that are necessary for clarity and completeness. Be sure to check your response for errors in grammar, spelling, and punctuation.

Writing for Pleasure and Insight

Even though our focus has been on scientific writing, in this chapter we have explored related types of writing, including writing for conferences (oral and poster presentations), the Web, and essay exams. Way back in chapter 1, I presented the six major categories of writing: expressive, exploratory, informative, scientific, literary, and persuasive (University of Maryland University College, 2005a). Writing is a powerful tool that humans exclusively possess, and we all have stories to tell or information to share. This tool analogy is not uncommon, as Zinsser (1988) wrote in his well-known book *Writing to Learn:*

> Writing is a tool that enables people in every discipline to wrestle facts and ideas. It's a physical activity, unlike reading. Writing requires us to operate some kind of mechanism—pencil, pen, typewriter, word processor—for getting our thoughts on paper. It compels us by the repeated effort of language to go after those thoughts and to organize them and present them clearly. It forces us to keep asking, "Am I saying what I want to say?" (p. 49)

As you think more broadly about writing, I encourage you to explore the beauty and simplicity of writing as a creative and insightful means of self-expression. Although you may not find joy in scientific writing at first, with practice it can actually happen. Pursue other avenues of writing that are more pleasurable for you—perhaps writing short stories, working on a family genealogy, or writing your own science fiction. Writing is an important creative outlet for human beings; even scientific writing, in the way that information is combined and hypotheses are formed and tested, is in its own way creative.

In addition to writing for pleasure, insight, and inspiration, physical and mental health professionals use writing exercises as a method to heal (Gaschler, 2007). In a classic study by Pennebaker, Kiecolt-Glaser, and Glaser (1988), 50 healthy undergraduate students wrote about either traumatic events or superficial topics for 20 minutes a day, 3 to 4 days in a row, for 6 weeks. The results indicated that students writing about traumatic events reported improved mood and fewer illnesses than those in the control group. Other studies have shown that this type of expressive writing can reduce doctor visits, improve grades, and lead to other positive outcomes (Slatcher & Pennebaker, 2006).

Additionally, patients experiencing fibromyalgia (a disorder involving muscle pain, stiffness, and fatigue), when instructed to write about personal traumatic events, experienced short-term psychological and health benefits as compared with a control group (Broderick, Junghaenel, & Schwartz, 2005). Stanton et al. (2002) also found that patients with early stage breast cancer reduced medical visits when asked to express themselves emotionally by writing (as compared with controls). In another example of the beneficial effects of writing about stressful life experiences, Smyth, Stone, Hurewitz, and Kaell (1999) found that this type of writing reduced the symptoms of those with asthma or rheumatoid arthritis (a type of arthritis that leads to the destruction of the joints). Each of these studies included control groups that wrote about other topics, so it is not just the mere fact of writing that helps to relieve pain, but writing about stressful experiences and traumatic events.

Murray (2002) described a number of research efforts in which writing is used in controlled studies to help clients in therapy. Although daily logs, questionnaires, and journals have been used as therapeutic tools for some time, recent research has suggested that "writing about emotions and stress can boost immune functioning in patients with such illnesses as HIV/AIDS, asthma and arthritis" (para. 2). Part of this benefit comes from the way people use writing to interpret their experiences, including word choice, and this benefit appears to be greater than just a venting of emotions. Researchers do warn that writing about traumatic events can initially trigger distress and physical and emotional arousal, but like any other therapeutic technique, client progress should be monitored by a qualified therapist. That is, over time there should be stress relief and a chance of approach as demonstrated by the client's writing; otherwise, writing may be an ineffective tool.

Writing is but one characteristic that separates us from other species. The ability to communicate via writing is a quality and trait to be honored, accepted, and practiced. Make the time to write for yourself, as well as practicing your scientific writing in psychology. Remember that writing can lift our spirits and explore ideas and places worth exploring. I leave you with this Shakespearean sonnet about writing that expresses one's most intimate hopes:

> O! know, sweet love, I always write of you,
> And you and love are still my argument;
> So all my best is dressing old words new,
> Spending again what is already spent.

> —*William Shakespeare*, Sonnet 100

References

American Psychological Association. (2007). *Thesaurus of psychological index terms* (L. A. Gallagher, Ed.; 11th ed.). Washington, DC: Author.

American Psychological Association. (2010). *Publication manual of the American Psychological Association* (6th ed.). Washington, DC: Author.

American Psychological Association. (2012a). *APA style guide to electronic references* (6th ed.). Washington, DC: Author. Available from http://www.apa.org/pubs/books

American Psychological Association. (2012b). *PsycEXTRA fact sheet.* Retrieved from http://www.apa.org/pubs/data bases/psycinfo/index.aspx

American Psychological Association. (2012c). *PsycINFO database information.* Retrieved from http://www.apa.org/pubs/librarians/product-descriptions.aspx

Appelcline, K. (n.d.). *The elements of good storytelling.* Retrieved from http://www.skotos.net/articles/GoodStorytelling.html

Austin, J. T., & Calderon, R. F., (2006). Writing in APA style: Why and how. In F. T. L. Leong & J. T. Austin (Eds.), *The psychology research handbook: A guide for graduate students and research assistants* (2nd ed., pp. 345–359). Thousand Oaks, CA: Sage.

Baker, D. S., & Henrichsen, L. (2002). *APA reference style: Introduction.* Retrieved from Brigham Young University Web site: http://linguistics.byu.edu/faculty/henrichsenl/apa/APA02.html

Ballon, R. (2005). *Blueprint for screenwriting: A complete writer's guide to story structure and character development.* Mahwah, NJ: Erlbaum.

Bellquist, J. E. (1993). *A guide to grammar and usage for psychology and related fields.* Hillsdale, NJ: Erlbaum.

Bem, D. J. (2004). Writing the empirical journal article. In J. M. Darley, M. P. Zanna, & H. L. Roediger III (Eds.), *The compleat academic: A career guide* (2nd ed., pp. 185–219). Washington, DC: American Psychological Association.

Bentley, M., Peerenboom, C. A., Hodge, F. W., Passano, E. B., Warren, H. C., & Washburn, M. F. (1929). Instructions in regard to preparation of manuscript. *Psychological Bulletin, 26,* 57–63. doi:10.1037/h0071487

Blumenthal, A. L. (1991). The intrepid Joseph Jastrow. In G. A. Kimble, M. Wetheimer, & C. White (Eds.), *Portraits of pioneers in psychology* (pp. 75–87). Washington, DC: American Psychological Association.

Bordens, K. S., & Abbott, B. B. (2004). *Research design and methods: A process approach* (5th ed.). Boston, MA: McGraw-Hill.

Brewer, B. W., Scherzer, C. B., Van Raalte, J. L., Petitpas, A. J., & Andersen, M. B. (2001). The elements of (APA) style: A survey of psychology journal editors. *American Psychologist, 56,* 266–267. doi:10.1037/0003-066X.56.3.266

Broderick, J. E., Junghaenel, D. U., & Schwartz, J. E. (2005). Written emotional expression produces health benefits in fibromyalgia patients. *Psychosomatic Medicine, 67,* 326–334. doi:10.1097/01.psy.0000156933.04566.bd

Brunsvold, L. (2003). *LEO thesis statement.* Retrieved from St. Cloud State University Web site: http://leo.stcloudstate.edu/acadwrite/thesistatement.html

Corbel, E. (2005). *Lesser-known editing and proofreading marks* [Cartoon]. Retrieved from: http://www.geist.com/articles/no-pringles/photos.html#275

Council of Writing Program Administrators, Purdue University. (2003). *Defining and avoiding plagiarism: The WPA statement on best practices* [Handout]. West Lafayette, IN: Author.

Crawford, H. J., & Christensen, L. B. (1995). *Developing research skills: A laboratory manual* (3rd ed.). Boston, MA: Allyn & Bacon.

Danya International, Inc. (2003). *Formulating a research question.* Retrieved from http://www.theresearchassistant.com/tutorial/2.asp

Dunn, J., Ford, K., Rewey, K. L., Juve, J. A., Weiser, A., & Davis, S. F. (2001). A modified presubmission checklist. *Psi Chi Journal of Undergraduate Research, 6,* 142–144.

Eisenberg, N. (2000). Writing a literature review. In R. J. Sternberg (Ed.), *Guide to publishing in psychology journals* (pp. 17–34). Cambridge, England: Cambridge University Press. doi:10.1017/CBO9780511 807862.003

Empire State College. (n.d.-a). *Developing a research question.* Retrieved from http://www.esc.edu/htmlpages/writerold/menus.htm

Empire State College. (n.d.-b). *Revising and proofreading.* Retrieved from http://www.esc.edu/esconline/across_esc/writerscomplex.nsf/ wholeshortlinks2/Revising?opendocument

Festinger, L. (1957). *A theory of cognitive dissonance.* Oxford, England: Row, Peterson.

Forrest, D. (n.d.). *How can I use PowerPoint more effectively?* Retrieved from Texas Tech University Teaching, Learning & Professional Development Center Web site: http://www.tlpd.ttu.edu/teach/TLTC% 20Teaching%20Resources/using_powerpoint.asp

Freimuth, M. (2008). *A self-scoring exercise on APA style and research language.* Santa Barbara, CA: The Fielding Graduate University.

Galvan, J. L. (2006). Guidelines for writing a first draft. *In writing literature reviews: A guide for students of the social and behavioral sciences* (3rd ed., pp. 81–90). Glendale, CA: Pyrczak.

Gaschler, K. (2007, August/September). The power of the pen. *Scientific American Mind,* 14–15. doi:10.1038/scientificamericanmind0807-14

Gottschalk, K., & Hjortshoj, K. (2004). *The elements of teaching writing: A resource for instructors in all disciplines.* Boston, MA: Bedford/St. Martin's.

Harris, R. A. (2005). *Using sources effectively: Strengthening your writing and avoiding plagiarism* (2nd ed.). Glendale, CA: Pyrczak.

Hibbard, C. S. (2001). *How to proofread your own writing.* Retrieved from Cypress Media Group Web site: http://cypressmedia.net/articles/ article/14/how_to_proofread_your_own_writing

Hiroshi, S. (1997). *What is Occam's razor?* Retrieved from University of California, Riverside, Web Site: http://www.math.ucr.edu/home/ baez/physics/General/occam.html

How experts communicate [Editorial]. (2000). *Nature Neuroscience, 3,* 97. doi:10.1038/72151

Jupitermedia Corporation. (2001). *Writing well for the Web: Overcoming the most common mistakes.* Retrieved from http://www.webreference. com/content/writing/overcome.html

Karlin, N. J. (2000). Creating an effective conference presentation. *Eye on Psi Chi, 4*(2), 26–27.

Kemlo, L., & Morgan, B. (2004). *Writing a literature review.* Retrieved from RMIT University Web site: http://www.rmit.edu.au/browse/ Current%20students%2FLibrary%2FGuides,%20tutorials%20and %20classes%2FLibrary%20guide%20to%20literature%20review/

Kendall, P. C., Silk, J. S., & Chu, B. C. (2000). Introducing your research report: Writing the introduction. In R. J. Sternberg (Ed.), *Guide to publishing in psychology journals* (pp. 41–57). Cambridge, England: Cambridge University Press. doi:10.1017/CBO9780511807862.005

Kendall-Tackett, K. A. (2007). *How to write for a general audience: A guide for academics who want to share their knowledge with the world and have fun doing it.* Washington, DC: American Psychological Association.

Kennedy, J. (n.d.). *Preparing a laboratory report in APA format.* Retrieved from http://www.psywww.com/tipsheet/labrep.htm

Kidd, S., Meyer, C. L., & Olesko, B. M. (2000). *An instructor's guide to electronic databases of indexed professional literature.* Statesboro, GA: Society for the Teaching of Psychology.

Kirk, E. E. (1996). *Evaluating information found on the Internet.* Retrieved from Johns Hopkins University Web site: http://guides.library. jhu.edu/evaluatinginformation

Landau, J. D. (2003). *Understanding and preventing plagiarism.* Retrieved from http://www.psychologicalscience.org/teaching/tips/tips_ 0403.cfm

Landrum, R. E. (2003). Graduate admissions in psychology: Transcripts and the effect of withdrawals. *Teaching of Psychology, 30,* 323–325. doi:10.1207/S15328023TOP3002_11

Landrum, R. E., & Davis, S. F. (2007). *The psychology major: Career options and strategies for success* (3rd ed.). Upper Saddle River, NJ: Prentice-Hall.

Landrum, R. E., & Muench, D. M. (1994). Assessing students' library skills and knowledge: The Library Research Strategies Questionnaire. *Psychological Reports, 75,* 1619–1628.

Langston, W. (2002). *Research methods laboratory manual for psychology.* Pacific Grove, CA: Wadsworth.

Lipkewich, A. E. (2001). *ABC's of the writing process—Editing.* Retrieved from Westmount School Web site: http://www.angelfire.com/wi/ writingprocess/editing.html

Lunsford, A. A. (n.d.). *EasyWriter.* Retrieved from http://bcs. bedfordstmartins.com/easywriter3e/20errors/default.asp

Lyons, K. (2005). *Write a literature review.* Retrieved from University of California, Santa Cruz, Web site: http://library.ucsc.edu/help/howto/ write-a-literature-review

Margulies, J. (2002, October 2). President of NY's Hamilton College steps down amid controversy over speech. *Chronicle of Higher Education.* Retrieved from http://chronicle.com/article/President-of-NYs-Hamilton/116644/

Martin, D. W. (1991). *Doing psychology experiments* (3rd ed.). Pacific Grove, CA: Brooks/Cole.

Mathews, B. S. (2004). Gray literature: Resources for locating unpublished research. *College & Research Libraries News, 65*(3), 125–129.

Mayer, R. E. (2001). *Multimedia learning.* New York, NY: Cambridge University Press.

McCarthy, M., & Pusateri, T. P. (2006). Teaching students to use electronic databases. In W. Buskist & S. F. Davis (Eds.), *Handbook of the teaching of psychology* (pp. 107–111). Malden, MA: Blackwell. doi:10.1002/9780470754924.ch18

McConnell, P. (2000). *Writing a lab report.* Retrieved from http://staff.gps.edu/McConnell/Toolbox/labreport.htm

McCormick, K. (1994). "On a topic of your own choosing . . ." In J. Clifford & J. Schilb (Eds.), *Writing theory and critical theory* (pp. 33–52). New York, NY: Modern Language Association of America.

McGovern, G. (n.d.). *The Web Content Style Guide excerpt: Writing for the web: Part I.* Retrieved from http://www.gerrymcgovern.com/guide_write_01.htm

McGraw-Hill/Dushkin. (n.d.). *How to write term papers.* Retrieved from http://novella.mhhe.com/sites/0079876543/student_view0/research_center-999/research_papers30/how_to_write_term_papers.html

Merriam-Webster, Inc. (2007). *Proofreaders' marks.* Retrieved from http://www.merriam-webster.com/mw/table/proofrea.htm

Microsoft Corp. (2007). *What's new in Microsoft Office OneNote 2007.* Retrieved from http://office.microsoft.com/en-us/onenote-help/what-s-new-in-microsoft-office-onenote-2007-HA010032570.aspx

Miller, G. A. (1956). The magical number seven, plus or minus two: Some limits on our ability to process information. *Psychological Review, 63*(2), 81–97. doi:10.1037/h0043158

Miller, H. L., & Lance, C. L. (2006). Written and oral assignments. In W. Buskist & S. F. Davis (Eds.), *Handbook of the teaching of psychology* (pp. 259–264). Malden, MA: Blackwell. doi: 10.1002/9780470754924.ch44

Mindola Software. (2006). *Supernotecard for scriptwriting.* Retrieved from http://www.mindola.com/supernotecard-for-scriptwriting/

Mitchell, M. L., Jolley, J. M., & O'Shea, R. P. (2004). *Writing for psychology: A guide for students.* Belmont, CA: Wadsworth/Thomson Learning.

Montoya, S. A., Smit, D. J., & Landrum, R. E. (2000, May). *Withdrawals and student transcripts: Do they effect the graduate admissions process?* Paper presented at the 73rd annual meeting of the Midwestern Psychological Association, Chicago, IL.

Murray, B. (2002, June). Writing to heal. *Monitor on Psychology, 33*(6). Retrieved from http://www.apa.org/monitor/jun02/writing.aspx

Myers, D. G. (2007). Teaching psychological science through writing. *Teaching of Psychology, 34,* 77–84. doi:10.1080/00986280701291283

Nicol, A. A. M., & Pexman, P. M. (2010). *Displaying your findings: A practical guide for creating figures, posters, and presentations* (6th ed.). Washington, DC: American Psychological Association.

Nota Bene. (n.d.). *Nota Bene: Software for academic research & writing.* Retrieved from http://www.notabene.com/chart.html

Online Writing Laboratory. (2004). *Writing a research paper: Thesis or question.* Retrieved from Purdue University Web site: http://owl.english.purdue.edu/workshops/hypertext/ResearchW/strat.html

Pennebaker, J. W., Kiecolt-Glaser, J. K., & Glaser, R. (1988). Disclosure of traumas and immune function: Health implications for psychotherapy. *Journal of Consulting and Clinical Psychology, 56,* 239–245. doi:10.1037/0022-006X.56.2.239

Plonsky, M. (2006). *Psychology with style: A hypertext writing guide.* Retrieved from the University of Wisconsin—Stevens Point Web site: http://www4.uwsp.edu/psych/mp/APA/apa4b.htm

Price, M. (2002). Beyond "Gotcha!": Situating plagiarism in policy and pedagogy. *College Composition and Communication, 54,* 88–115. doi:10.2307/1512103

Psi Chi. (2007). *Sample poster arrangements.* Retrieved from http://www.psichi.org/conventions/samples.aspx

Reaves, C. (2004, October). *Teaching APA style to beginners* [Handout]. Best Practices in Teaching Research Methods and Statistics conference, Atlanta, GA.

Roediger, H. L. (2004, April). What should they be called? *APS Observer, 17.* Retrieved from http://www.psychologicalscience.org/observer/getArticle.cfm?id=1549

Roediger, H. L. (2007, June/July). Twelve tips for authors. *APS Observer, 20,* 39–41.

Salovey, P. (2000). Results that get results: Telling a good story. In R. J. Sternberg (Ed.), *Guide to publishing in psychology journals* (pp. 121–132). Cambridge, England: Cambridge University Press. doi:10.1017/CBO9780511807862.009

Scott, J. M., Koch, R. E., Scott, G. M., & Garrison, S. M. (2002). *The psychology student writer's manual* (2nd ed.). Upper Saddle River, NJ: Prentice Hall.

Scribe, A. (2012). *APA style quick study.* Retrieved from http://www. docstyles.com/apastudy.htm

Shadle, S. (2006, December). *Writing and citing workshop.* Presented by the Center for Teaching and Learning, Boise State University, Boise, ID.

Shertzer, M. (1986). *The elements of grammar.* New York, NY: Collier Books.

Silvia, P. J. (2007). *How to write a lot: A practical guide to productive academic writing.* Washington, DC: American Psychological Association.

Slatcher, R. B., & Pennebaker, J. W. (2006). How do I love thee? Let me count the words: The social effects of expressive writing. *Psychological Science, 17,* 660–664. doi:10.1111/j.1467-9280.2006.01762.x

Smith, R. A. (2000). Documenting your scholarship: Citations and references. In R. J. Sternberg (Ed.), *Guide to publishing in psychology journals* (pp. 146–158). Cambridge, England: Cambridge University Press. doi:10.1017/CBO9780511807862.011

Smyth, J. M., Stone, A. A., Hurewitz, A., & Kaell, A. (1999, April 14). Effects of writing about stressful experiences on symptom reduction in patients with asthma or rheumatoid arthritis. *JAMA, 281,* 1304–1309. doi:10.1001/jama.281.14.1304

SparkNotes. (2006). *Writing the rough draft.* Retrieved from http://www. sparknotes.com/college/admissions/page16.html

Stanton, A. L., Danoff-Burg, S., Sworowski, L. A., Collins, C. A., Branstetter, A. D., Rodriguez-Hanley, A.,...Austenfeld, J. L. (2002). Randomized, controlled trial of written emotional expression and benefit finding in breast cancer patients. *Journal of Clinical Oncology, 20,* 4160–4168. doi:10.1200/JCO.2002.08.521

Sternberg, R. J. (2000). Titles and abstracts: They only sound unimportant. In R. J. Sternberg (Ed.), *Guide to publishing in psychology journals* (pp. 37–40). Cambridge, England: Cambridge University Press. doi:10.1017/CBO9780511807862.004

Sternberg, R. J. (2005). *The psychologist's companion: A guide to scientific writing for students and researchers* (4th ed.). New York, NY: Cambridge University Press.

Strunk, W., Jr., & White, E. B. (1979). *The elements of style* (3rd ed.). New York, NY: Macmillan.

Szuchman, L. (2005). *Writing with style: APA style made easy* (3rd ed.). Belmont, CA: Wadsworth.

Texas A&M University. (2011). *Revising and proofreading.* Retrieved from University Writing Center Web site: http://writingcenter.tamu.edu/ 2005/how-to/revising-editing/revising-and-proofreading/

Trochim, W. M. K. (2001). *Research methods knowledge base* (2nd ed.). Cincinnati, OH: Atomic Dog.

TruTamil LLC. (2004). *ndxCards*. Retrieved from http://www.ndxcards.com

University of Arkansas at Little Rock. (2002). *UWC—Proofreading tips*. Retrieved from the Online Writing Lab Web site: http://ualr.edu/writingcenter/index.php/tips-for-effective-proofreading/

University of Maryland University College. (2005a). *Helping students avoid plagiarism*. Retrieved from http://www.umuc.edu/writingcenter/facultywriting/avoidingplagiarism.cfm

University of Maryland University College. (2005b). *Types of writing assignments*. Retrieved from http://www.umuc.edu/writingcenter/facultywriting/design_types.cfm

University of North Carolina at Chapel Hill. (n.d.). *Editing and proofreading*. Retrieved from the Writing Center Web site: http://writingcenter.unc.edu/resources/handouts-demos/citation/editing-and-proofreading

University of Richmond. (2010). *Types of writing in psychology*. Retrieved from the Writing Center Web site: http://writing2.richmond.edu/writing/wweb/psychology/types.html

University of Texas Learning Center. (2006). *Essay tests*. Retrieved from http://www.lifelearning.utexas.edu/l_essaytest.html

University of Washington. (2005). *Writing a psychology literature review*. Retrieved from the Psychology Writing Center Web site: http://www.psych.uw.edu/writingcenter/writingguides/pdf/litrev.pdf

University of Wisconsin—Madison Writing Center. (n.d.). *UW-Madison Writing Center writer's handbook*. Retrieved from http://writing.wisc.edu/Handbook/index.html

Van Wagenen, R. K. (1991). *Writing a thesis: Substance and style*. Upper Saddle River, NJ: Prentice Hall.

Vipond, D. (1993). *Writing and psychology: Understanding writing and its teaching from the perspective of composition studies*. Westport, CT: Praeger.

Warburton, J. (2005). *Literature reviews*. Retrieved from the University of Melbourne Web site: http://unimelb.libguides.com/content.php?pid=87165&search_terms=doing+literature+review

Watson, J. B. (1925). *Behaviorism*. New York, NY: People's Institute.

Woods, G. (2007). *Dummies: Notetaking on the computer*. Retrieved from http://www.dummies.com/how-to/content/notetaking-on-the-computer.html

Zinsser, W. (1988). *Writing to learn*. New York, NY: Harper & Row.

Index

About the Author

R. Eric Landrum, PhD, is a professor of psychology at Boise State University, Idaho. He received his PhD in cognitive psychology (with an emphasis in quantitative methodology) from Southern Illinois University, Carbondale, in 1989. His research interests center on the study of educational issues, identifying those conditions that best facilitate student success (broadly defined). He has made over 200 professional presentations at conferences and published 17 books or book chapters and over 60 professional articles in scholarly, peer-reviewed journals. His work has appeared in journals such as *Teaching of Psychology, College Teaching, Educational and Psychological Measurement, Journal of College Student Development, College Student Journal,* and *Psychological Reports.* He has worked with more than 200 undergraduate research assistants and in 16 years at Boise State, he has taught over 10,000 students.

Dr. Landrum is the coeditor and author of two chapters in *Protecting Human Subjects: Departmental Subject Pools and Institutional Review Boards* (1999) and lead author (with Stephen F. Davis) of *The Psychology Major: Career Options and Strategies for Success* (3rd ed., 2007). He is a member of the American Psychological Association (fellow; Division 2, Society for the Teaching of Psychology), the Midwestern Psychological Association, and the Rocky

Mountain Psychological Association. He is an award-winning teacher (Associated Students of Boise State University Outstanding Faculty Member Award, 1994 and 2005; Boise State University Foundation Scholars Outstanding Teacher Award, 2002) and researcher (Social Sciences & Public Affairs Tenured Research Award, 2004). At Boise State University, Dr. Landrum teaches courses in General Psychology (in the classroom and online), Introduction to the Psychology Major, Statistical Methods, Research Methods, and Psychological Measurements. He has served as national president of the Council of Teachers of Undergraduate Psychology and works with Psi Chi both locally and regionally. He served as department chair from 1996–2000 and again from 2005–2006.